A Colonel & A Cowboy

A Colonel & A Cowboy
Mission, Mindset, Process
Strategies of the Elite

J. Craig Flowers & Stran T Smith

©2024 All Rights Reserved. No portion of this book may be reproduced, stored in a retrieval system, or transmitted in any form or by any means—electronic, mechanical, photocopy, recording, scanning, or other—except for brief quotations in critical reviews or articles without the prior permission of the author.

Published by Game Changer Publishing

Paperback ISBN: 978-1-965653-58-6
Hardcover ISBN: 978-1-965653-59-3
Digital ISBN: 978-1-965653-60-9

www.GameChangerPublishing.com

DEDICATION

A special thank you to all those who encouraged us both to write a book. Stran and I discussed our book's Dedication in depth. From teammates, friends, coaches, mentors, and family.

I was close to both of my grandmothers in San Antonio, Texas. They helped raise me as a little boy. I remember their hugs and kind smiles. My uncle was like a big brother, especially while my father served in Vietnam. Dad, aka "Coach," spent countless hours playing catch and pushing me in athletics (now I realize how tired he must have been, yet he still made time). I love both my brothers, Chris and Cliff—we have become even closer in our later years.

To my mom, Nancy O. Flowers, my wife Beth, aka "Miss Beth," my sister Carrie Leigh Calvert, and our three daughters—Kathleen, Annie, and Julia. Thank you all for your steadfast belief, love, and support. May God bless our armed forces, the American Cowboy, and our Great nation.

–J. Craig Flowers

Very first and foremost, I want to thank my Lord and Savior for allowing me to represent Him. My prayer is that I serve Him as Father with excellence and humility and reflect Him in all I do.

I've had the privilege of being raised by some of the best, strongest men who led by example and, with servants' hearts, molded me into the man, competitor, leader, and man of faith I am today. I want to thank the most influential men in my life: my granddad, Will T, my dad, Clifton, and my big brother, Smitty, who raised me with a foundation of faith, fortitude, and reliance. This book is for them and my two heroes, my boys, Stone T & Scout. I am more proud of you both than you'll ever know.

As much as the men in my life have led me by example, it's the matriarchs in my life who have molded my character and helped forge my spirit. I'd like to especially dedicate this book to them. Without their love and leadership, I would not be here today. To my mom, Judy, and my wife, Jennifer—your unquestionable support and belief in me made me feel like I could walk on water. You gave me the confidence to believe there's no mountain I can't conquer, no matter how low the valleys are. Jennifer, you give me grace when I need it and inspire me daily. None of this story would have happened without you by my side. To my sisters, Susy, Shari & Sealy—thank you for being my loudest cheerleaders. I can always count on your support and love.

Lastly, this book is dedicated to our perfect completion, Selah Trinity, who keeps me motivated to be better every day. I love you all.

–Stran T Smith

Read This First

Just to say thanks for buying and reading our book, we would like to give you some bonus items!

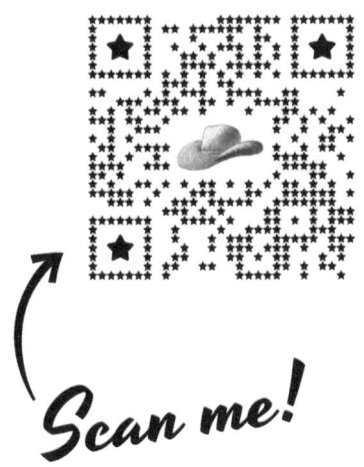

A Colonel & A Cowboy

Mission, Mindset, Process

Strategies of the Elite

J. Craig Flowers & Stran T Smith

www.GameChangerPublishing.com

ACKNOWLEDGMENTS

"Psalms 37:23 tells us, 'The steps of a good man are ordered by the Lord, and He delights in His way.' When I think about what it means to be a good man, I think of men like Stran Smith and Colonel Craig Flowers. Men who are devoted to faith, family, and building a better world for the next generation. A better world tomorrow will not happen by accident. It will require an effective game plan and the courage to diligently carry that plan out every day. In the pages of this book, A Colonel & A Cowboy you will not only read the strategies that make a better world possible but learn from the firsthand experiences of men who possessed enough grit and determination to refuse to quit until the mission was accomplished and the goal achieved. No matter the challenges you are facing, goals you are pursuing, or motivation you need, this book contains the road map that will get you there. You will be encouraged, challenged, and inspired, but most of all, you will become a part of the elite few who are willing to make the commitment to keep moving forward, always believing that better is possible."

– **Matthew Hagee**, Lead Pastor Cornerstone Church, San Antonio, Texas

"I have had the pleasure of observing Colonel(Retired) Craig Flowers for the past 35 years. Simply stated, he is the "real deal": authentic, purpose-driven, and incredibly inspirational. As a true student of leadership in high-performing outfits, he shares his vast experience in this wonderful primer."

– **Lieutenant General (Retired) Lawson W. Magruder III**
Author of *A Soldier's Journey Living His Why: Inspired by a Little Green Book* and Co-author of *Of Their Own Accord: A Company of Army Rangers Changing Lives in Changing Times.*

"They say never meet your heroes because they might disappoint you, but Stran's character wouldn't allow that. Our relationship has gone from me looking up to him when I was younger and just starting out, to us being friends, and now getting to call him family. Whether it's in life or in the arena, when the chips are down, he's one of the guys I want in my corner. This book will not only give you a blueprint for how to be a champion, but how to be a champion who can look at themselves in the mirror every morning and like what they see. There are no shortcuts in life, but if you want to get to your goals faster, the strategies in this book will help you avoid pitfalls and discover the tactics that'll help make you a champion and a leader."

– **Trevor Brazile**, 26-time World Champion Cowboy

"Emerging leaders in our organization received a solid foundation built on strategy and integrity under the watchful eye and personal mentorship of Craig. His unique training and experience are brought to life through storytelling and his ability to inspire. Craig is an elite leader and I'm grateful to have experienced his dedication to the Mission, Mindset, Process approach over our decade long friendship."

– **Markham R McKnigh**t, Regional Executive Chairman, Gallagher & Co.

"I've been friends with Stran Smith for 35 years, and I can attest that Stran's character, principle, and work ethic are a direct correlation to his success, both as world champion tie-down roper and an entrepreneur and rancher.

I've been around a lot of champions and successful businessmen, but what sets Stran apart is what a truly great human being, husband, and father he is, and I know that that comes from those same principles - ones that he shares in this book. For 35 years, with Stran, I've gotten to see that sometimes, the good guy wins. I'm proud to be his friend and one of his biggest supporters. I haven't yet met the Colonel, but Stran's endorsement of him means more to me than his impressive resume. I can't wait for everyone to read this book! Stran Smith for President!"

– **Ty Murray**, 9-time World Champion Cowboy, Co-Founder of the Professional Bull Riders and National Day of the Horse

"Craig is the epitome of a military colonel. From his career and life experiences, he leads by example and coaches to making well-thought-out decisions. He's a great motivator for anyone looking to be the best they can be, whether in life or business. And Stran Smith's record speaks for itself."

– **Johnny Carrabba**, Founder of The Johnny Carrabba Family of Restaurants

"I worked with COL Flowers for 5 years. He was very easy to work with, down to earth, and very respectful of his staff. I always thought of him as a mentor. I learned a lot from him; some of these things I still use today thirteen years after retirement."

– **Mark T. Judson**, Facilities Manager (ret,) West Point

"Leadership isn't some abstract set of tenets for these two men, but rather a suite of core values and meticulously applied principles that they embody and put to work each and every day. With an artesian well of life and wisdom between them, Smith and Flowers draw upon their vast array of experiences leading, serving, competing, and teaching at the highest levels of the military, professional sports, and business to share what really makes successful leaders tick. Grounded by their faith, uncompromising in their self-discipline, and inspired by service to God and Country, the Colonel and the Cowboy offer a pragmatic and clear-eyed view of leadership that is simply second to none."

– **Carter Smith**, Retired Executive Director, Texas Parks and Wildlife Department

"Colonel Craig Flowers is a true leader. His life story is incredible and molded him into an exceptional human and leader. He is authentic, bold, and a great storyteller. His stories are motivating and entertaining.

– **Dave Bailiff**, NCAA College Football Coach

"From my conversations with Stran throughout the years, to watching him share his faith at cowboy church in Las Vegas during the NFR, to spending time around his family, I've always been both impressed and inspired by my friend Stran, and I feel the same way about his new book, 'A Colonel & A Cowboy.' After reading it, I'm sure you'll feel the same."

– **Aaron Watson**, Country Music Singer/Songwriter

Foreword

For over 20 years, I have had the privilege of being married to Stran, a man whose unique characteristics of hard work and leadership have always been at the core of who he is and are just a few of the things that I love about him. Everything he undertakes is done with a level of excellence that is inspiring—and sometimes humbling. His relentless pursuit of his goals, combined with an unwavering integrity, has always set him apart.

It's not that Stran trained to be that way... it is simply who he is. I believe that it is part of his spiritual gifting. Time and again, I've seen him choose the "harder right over the easier wrong" (West Point Cadet Prayer), even when it cost him a competitive advantage. His story is a true testament to his steadfast moral compass and deep-rooted values.

When we first met Colonel Craig Flowers, it was obvious that what he was teaching was what Stran had been living out all these years. Our boys had been accepted into Air It Out, an elite developmental football academy that combines football skills with faith, character, and leadership development. "The Colonel," as we call him (even though he'd prefer to simply be "Craig"), teaches the character and leadership development sessions.

What a life-changing blessing to get the opportunity for these accomplished men to speak wisdom on every level to our sons. All the wisdom you try to impart as a parent is suddenly resonating, as it is coming from collegiate and Super Bowl champions and an Army colonel from West Point. We went for the football but came back for the character and leadership development.

It was in the parenting breakout sessions that I watched a very special friendship develop between my husband and the Colonel. You would think they are a very unlikely pair, but at their core, their foundations of faith, work ethic, and pursuit of excellence aligned seamlessly. In fact, I was struck by how, without knowing each other, they ran their camps and clinics with such similarity. Both men aren't just teaching the fundamentals of skill and technique—they teach about leadership, character, and faith. They also don't just teach the students. Parents are taught intentional, tactical parenting strategies emphasizing their role in their child's character development.

May I just brag for a minute? The Colonel and the Cowboy are two accomplished humans. The Colonel is a distinguished Army officer and West Point baseball coach who works closely with NCAA and professional coaches, directors of athletics, educators, CEOs, and leaders of Fortune 500 companies across the country, imparting his expertise and strategic insights.

After Stran's World Championship run, his career evolved into opportunities to enlighten others, from hosting Elevation Sunday during the WNFR (the World Series of Rodeo) for 15 years to his nationwide speaking engagements. His popular, nationally published monthly article, *Down the Line with Stran Smith*, spurred a weekly social media video, *Tack Room Talks*, that has further solidified his mission of challenging and encouraging others.

As their friendship grew, the idea of teaching together started to form. They would flippantly say in passing, "When are we going to write a book together?" When Game Changer Publishing approached them, the idea became a reality quickly. I then watched as these two men lived out the strategies and processes they are about to share with you in this book, and it has been truly magical.

Not only am I excited for the world to learn from this book, but I am also thrilled for you to hear their special synergy on their upcoming national podcast series, *A Colonel and a Cowboy with a Little Bit of Jen* (yes, they are trying to rope me in). We keep saying that they are an unlikely pair, but these two friends have such a unique dynamic when teaching together: They seem to anticipate each other's thoughts and finish each other's sentences as if their words were scripted.

I am so blessed to have these men in my life, not only living these principles out daily and passing them on to all of our children, but what a blessing that they believe in people enough to analyze and create a process for "anyone willing" to become the elite that God created them to be. It is truly a service to a cause.

I hope you are as blessed by reading this book as I have been to live it.

– *Jennifer Douglas-Smith*

Table of Contents

Chapter 1 – Change-of-Mission Mindset 1

Chapter 2 – Great to Elite: The 4% 25

Chapter 3 – How the Most Elite in the World Train and Behave to Win 39

Chapter 4 – Character Reps vs. Physical Reps 55

Chapter 5 – Know, Care, Then Challenge 61

Chapter 6 – Processes to Trust: The Decision-Making Process and the After-Action Review 77

Chapter 7 – Doing Discipline 89

Chapter 8 – How We Learn 101

Chapter 9 – Can They, Will They, Will Others? 111

Chapter 10 – Service and Leadership 119

Chapter 11 – Ego Is a Distraction: A Sense of Humor Is a Competitive Edge 129

Chapter 12 – What Field Are You Playing In? 139

Chapter 13 – Her Name Is Destiny 147

Conclusion (Chapter 14) 161

Rodeo Glossary 165

NOTE TO READER: This book includes the "voices" of both Craig and Stran. To help follow the story, we've included visual cues when the voice changes:

An Eagle for Craig

And a Cowboy Hat for Stran

We hope this enhances your reading experience.

CHAPTER 1

Change-of-Mission Mindset

"All members of the special operations community have a very unique way of behaving. One trait is a Change of Mission Mindset. The moment something fundamentally new occurs during a mission or operation, they change their mindset, their focus."
–J. Craig Flowers, U.S. Army Colonel, retired

• • •

BLUF (Bottom Line Up-Front): Without emotion and because of trust, when the mission changes due to unexpected, often sudden facts, the elite communicate and execute.

• • •

I'm going to start my story in December 1995. I was 25 years old, had just graduated from college, and was coming off of my rookie season as a professional rodeo cowboy. I had really wanted to get my degree before I took off and rodeoed full-time, so I was happy to be able to do both in 1995.

Life at this point was really good. It was my first year to rodeo full-time professionally, and I qualified for the National Finals—rodeo's Super Bowl—held in Vegas every December. I decided to drive out by myself. I never minded long drives alone… they gave me time to think, focus, and free myself from distractions.

Before the ten days of competition even start, there's so much to do. You have to get there about a week in advance to meet with sponsors, check-in, go to required contestant rehearsals and meetings, and get the livestock prepared. Once the actual rodeo starts, you compete every night for a chance at the go-around money, which gets added to what you've earned throughout the year. The guy who wins the most money from the year plus the NFR is the world champion. The one who has the fastest time of the 10 rounds combined at the NFR wins the average, which is a big payday. More money is paid out in one NFR round than about 90% of the rodeos throughout the year, but it's also a marathon of physical strength and mental toughness. It's every cowboy's dream to just make it there, and in December of '95, I was headed out there for the first time.

I'd been there before as a spectator but never as a contestant, so you can imagine the excitement I felt when I got up at about five o'clock in the morning for the 14-hour drive. I had a brand new Chevrolet four-door truck and a sponsor trailer. I had just recently signed my endorsement deal with Cinch Jeans, which was one of their very first. I'm telling you, I couldn't have been any higher in life than what I was at that time.

On the way to Vegas, I stopped in Kingman, Arizona, to get some gas. It was about four or five o'clock in the afternoon, and I had been driving all day long. I'd had a great drive, listening to cassette tapes. However, instead of jamming away to the latest from Garth, George, or even Pearl Jam, I pumped myself up with the likes of Charles Stanley and John Hagee preaching. I was wired, fired, and inspired.

While I was filling up with diesel, I decided to call home and check in because my granddad hadn't been feeling very good. He was my biggest fan. If you look up the definition of a cowboy in the dictionary, it should be a picture of my granddad. He's actually my namesake. His name was Will T, and my name is Stran T. There's no bigger roping fan in the history of roping than he was. He was a true blue cowboy and a true blue fan of roping. He probably turned out more calves for me and helped me practice more than anybody.

So, there I was, fired up and high on all the great wisdom I'd been listening to, ready to talk to my number one fan for a little more inspiration. I picked up the gas station pay phone to place a collect call to my parents' house back in Tell, Texas. My mother answered and said, "Stran, I have some bad news."

"What's wrong, Mom?" I asked.

"Papa passed away this morning."

I was devastated. Ever since I had started roping, the only thing my granddad had been living for was to watch me rope at the National Finals. In my dreams, I always saw Papa right there at the NFR with me. After he had a stroke and it was clear that he wasn't going to be able to travel, my parents went to great lengths to set it up so that he would be able to watch me in real time via satellite. Back then, the rounds were broadcast on ESPN2, but not until after the performance was over, so this was a big deal at the time.

My mom told me that when Papa was lying in the hospital, he was kind of delirious before he died and said, "Can't they get that calf in the chute?"

"What's wrong, Papa?" they asked him. "What's wrong?"

"They're trying to get this calf in the chute, and they can't get him in the chute to let Stran rope." He had been dreaming about watching me rope at the National Finals Rodeo.

The fact that he never got to see his dream come to fruition added a whole new level to the heartbreak of losing my papa. The timing couldn't have been worse. Suddenly, I wasn't headed to Vegas just to live out my cowboy dreams.

Change of Mission

Now I had a bigger mission: to rope the best I could to honor my papa. As hard as it was to turn my focus from my heartache back to the job at hand, I had peace knowing that Papa was rejoicing in heaven, free from pain and suffering, and I have a pretty good feeling that he got to watch that NFR from the best seat in the house.

Up to this point in my life, I had never really suffered any kind of loss. I didn't have a lot of experience with grief or even going through hard things. Despite this, I actually did well in the Finals. I placed in seven of the ten go-rounds that year and actually won the sixth go-round. That's a big deal out there. You take the victory lap in front of thousands of cheering fans in the Thomas & Mack Center and get a go-around buckle and, of course, a nice paycheck. It's especially challenging for a rookie to walk in there for the first time and not be overwhelmed. The lights, the crowd, the energy... it can all be a lot. So, I was proud that I was able to overcome all the rookie jitters and grief from losing my papa and make a nice showing out there. I felt like he would've been proud.

One of the highlights of that year at the Finals for me was Shawn. I'd always known Shawn McMullen; we'd been friends, but at the Finals, we just kind of hit it off and went from being friendly acquaintances to more like brothers. You're always looking for somebody to be in your corner, on your team, one of your guys. Shawn turned into that guy for me.

At the Finals that year, Shawn had a chance to win the World Championship, and it came down to the last calf. I was standing in the box with him, and I was as nervous as a cat because this was the achievement of a lifetime. Shawn had been close a couple of times to winning a World Championship, but the title had eluded him. That year, it was gonna come down to the tenth go-round. He needed to tie his calf in less than seven seconds, but he didn't get it done. However, the bond that Shawn and I created that year was worth more to me than a gold buckle.

During that week in Vegas, Shawn asked me, "Who are you going to rodeo with next year?"

"I don't really have anybody," I told him. I was very selective about who I traveled with, and it's really hard to find guys who have the same goals and habits. Most guys who are roping for a living have the same goals, but there's a big difference in everyone's processes and approach to winning.

"Want to come with me?" he said. "Let's hook up."

And that's how Shawn McMullen became my traveling partner, best friend, and brother, and we were determined to set 1996 on fire.

If you've never seen the movie *The Ghost and the Darkness*, it's about two lions in Africa who go on a rampage together. I felt like that was us. We were truly on each other's team. We rooted for each other. We pulled for each other. We rode each other's horses. We built each other up. When one of us was facing a challenge, the other lifted him up, and when one of us won, we celebrated like both of us had. It was such a great partnership because Shawn was a shoot-from-the-hip kind of guy, whereas I was a strategic planner. I did things for us out in front, but when we needed to make a change on the fly, Shawn was in his element and helped me navigate those ropes. He was never on time, but he never had a bad day or a worry in the world. He kept me from being too tightly wound, and I kept him from getting too far into the weeds.

We flew a lot back then, especially Southwest, and many times, we sprinted onto the plane just as they were shutting the door. This was back before all the extra security, when you wouldn't get yourself declared a national security threat for running like a crazy man through an airport. Shawn and I were having a ball. We were both in the top ten rodeo standings. We had life by the tail, literally, two young guys at the top of their game. We had endorsements coming from left and right—people wanting us to advertise for them, promote for them, model for them, do all these things. We were two single guys living out their dreams. It's hard to even describe how much fun we were having.

On August 16, 1996, we were at the rodeo in Canby, Oregon, three-fourths of the way through the season. We were both in the top ten in the world, and the top 15 go to the National Finals. That night, Shawn did well, but I didn't. Afterward, he went to the sponsor's tent and made his rounds, signing autographs, shaking hands, and kissing babies. I went back to the trailer, unsaddled the horses, and got things ready to roll because I knew we had an all-night drive to get to the rodeo the next day in Heppner, Oregon.

After I got the rig ready to go, I went to bed in the living quarters of the trailer. Shawn had just bought a brand-new F-350 Ford Dually. It was gold—the first gold truck I'd ever seen. We got a great deal from one of my sponsors, Waylon Long, at 2L Custom Trucks, and I'm telling you, it was the coolest, pimped-out-est truck you've ever seen. He had all-wood consoles and big captain's chairs.

The trailer had full living quarters, a couch that pulled out into a full-size bed, and a kitchenette. It was a Sundowner, a gooseneck trailer. Sundowner was one of the first trailers that had a king-size bed up in the nose so you could sleep perpendicular to the highway. Later on, this quite possibly could have been one of the things that saved my life. But when I crawled up into the king-size bed and lay down sideways, I had no idea.

I cranked the generator and got into bed around 10:30. I don't usually fall asleep instantly, so I lay there, a little restless, silently willing Shawn to hurry up and quit politicking or chasing another cute girl so we could GO. This was before you could send a text or make a phone call. For all I knew, if I got up and went to look for him, I'd miss him, and then we'd be even further behind.

Well, one sponsorship event turned into another sponsorship event, which maybe turned into a little post-rodeo dance, so we didn't get out of there at a very good hour. I was about three-fourths asleep when I finally heard the horses getting on the trailer, and I knew we were fixing to leave. Well, Shawn knew me well enough to know that I was probably agitated that we were leaving at that hour. True to form, he opened the door of the trailer, thinking I was asleep. I wasn't, but I also wasn't fully awake. He started saying my name over and over again in a sing-song voice. I stubbornly pretended to be asleep until he finally gave up and left the trailer, laughing, still saying my name over and over.

Shawn got in the passenger seat of the gold truck, and as we pulled out of the fairgrounds, he rolled his window down and continued hollering my name all through town. I fell asleep laughing at his antics. You couldn't stay mad at Shawn; he always had a way about him like that.

We had a young man from Australia, Jared, who was helping us drive that summer. We had a deal where we always wanted to make sure somebody was up there with Jared to keep him awake and keep him company. So, we rolled out of Canby with me asleep in the nose of the trailer on the king-size bed, Jared driving, and Shawn riding shotgun.

It seemed like I had only been asleep for five minutes, but in reality, it was hours later, between two and three o'clock in the morning. I remember hearing the brakes just for an instant and then this huge crash. If I had been sleeping like you normally do, with my head toward the front, I might have broken my neck. Instead, my whole body hit the cabinets at the front of the trailer, spreading out the impact. That crash was one of the loudest noises I've ever heard. I didn't know if we had run into somebody in front of us or what had happened.

I rolled onto my back and braced myself against the top of the trailer because I could feel we were still going really fast. As the crash continued, a connector in the trailer broke loose. Sparks flew, metal crunched on metal, and I bounced around like a pinball.

It felt like we traveled for five minutes, but it wasn't more than 20 seconds before we finally came to a stop. I just had a pair of shorts on—no shirt, no shoes, no socks, nothing. But my adrenaline was surging, so I didn't think about any of that as I jumped out of the trailer and ran to the pickup. Every light in the truck had been knocked out.

We had just filled up with diesel before leaving that afternoon. I wasn't thinking clearly, but in my mind, I knew I had to get them out of this truck because it was fixing to catch on fire and might blow up. Now, I knew diesel doesn't explode, but at the time, this irrational fear was telling me that I needed to get them out of the truck.

That beautiful gold truck was completely crushed like a sardine can. There was no front. There was no motor. There were no front doors. It was a four-door pickup, and everything was mashed back into the second row. I ran around to the driver's side of the truck and saw Jared in the back seat. The crash had knocked him over the top of the captain's chair.

He was conscious, and I said, "Jared, are you okay?" He told me that all his teeth were knocked out, but other than that, he was okay, and he agreed to let me help him out. There was blood everywhere from his teeth being knocked out, but other than that, he seemed to be all right. I pulled him out of the truck and carried him to the other side of the interstate to get him safely away from where I was sure there would be a fire. There was no traffic. They said later on that it was one of the darkest nights of the year. To this day, when I think about that night, my core memory is of the absolute darkness all around me. I laid Jared down in the road ditch, and after making sure that he was as okay as he could be, I ran back to the pickup to get Shawn out.

Shawn was lying in the center of the back seat. The impact had knocked both of them into the back of the truck. He looked like he was asleep. Unlike Jared, there was no blood. He was lying on top of the console, and I put my arms underneath him and told him, "You're going to have to help me." I thought he was still asleep. I couldn't believe he could sleep through a wreck like that. I kept talking to him, asking him to help me help him. Then I looked at his right ear and saw that the bottom of his right earlobe had been ripped off. I remember looking at that and saying, "Oh, bud, your earlobe was ripped off. You're gonna look like you've had an earring. Do you know how much heck you're gonna catch from everybody?"

I was laughing and talking to him, teasing him like he'd been teasing me just a few hours earlier. I was still trying to move him when something told me to wait. So, I checked to see if I could feel him breathing or feel his pulse or something. I didn't, but I had so much adrenaline flowing that I wasn't really in my right mind.

At about that time, a truck came from the other direction on the interstate. I could see they had a trailer on and were trying to stop. I ran after it, knowing I needed help. When they stopped, I ran to the driver's side and asked, "Do y'all have a phone?"

"Yeah," they said.

"Call 9-1-1, please," I told them. "We've just been in a wreck. Shawn's still in the truck, and I can't get him out."

I ran back to the wreck while they called for help, and when I got back to Shawn, there was somebody there. I didn't know at the time, but he was an off-duty EMS worker. I ran up to him and asked him to help me get Shawn out.

He sent me back to check on Jared, which I did, and then I immediately ran back to implore the guy to help me get Shawn out.

"No," he said, "let's leave him right where he's at. We don't need to move him. Do you have a blanket? Go get a blanket, something to cover him up."

I raced into the trailer to find a blanket.

When we had filled up with diesel, we had also stocked our refrigerator with drinks and food, which were now all over the trailer. It looked like a bomb of drinks, sandwich meat, steaks, and everything else we'd bought had gone off in there. I crawled through it all, grabbed a blanket off the bed, and took it back to the off-duty EMS guy.

"Listen," he said, "the ambulance just got here, and they're taking your friend. Why don't you go over there and help them?"

I ran over to the ambulance, and the EMS paramedic there asked me if I had been in the wreck. He wanted to check me out. As he did, it hit me again that Shawn was still in the truck. I was starting to lose my cool, begging everyone there to just get Shawn out of the truck. That's when one of the emergency responders turned to me and said, "He didn't make it."

I stared at him. "What? What are you talking about?"

"I'm sorry. I didn't know you didn't know. Your friend didn't make it."

"What's that mean?" I asked.

"I'm sorry," he said again.

I was stunned. I just didn't know what had happened. There wasn't a scratch on Shawn, aside from the ripped earlobe. How could he be gone just like that?

When I was able to catch my breath, my first thought was, "I gotta call my mom. I gotta call my mom."

I borrowed somebody's phone and called my mom. By this time, it was about four o'clock in the morning in Texas. No good phone calls come at that time of day. My mom answered the phone and said, "What's wrong, baby?"

"I'm okay," I said

"Well, thank the Lord. Is everything alright?"

"Nah. Shawn didn't make it, Mom."

She started crying. "I'm so sorry."

After talking to her for another minute, I hung up the phone. Then I called Shawn's mom and dad. That was the hardest phone call I have ever made.

We found out later that we'd been hit head-on by a drunk driver driving the wrong way down the interstate with her headlights off. She was two and a half times over the legal limit. Even in our fancy, state-of-the-art rig, we didn't stand a chance. She was killed in the accident as well.

After that, I just went numb. I couldn't feel anything physically. Later on, I guess months, maybe even years later, they realized that I might have broken my neck in the wreck and didn't know it. My body and mind went on autopilot after that. I couldn't sleep. I couldn't eat. It was like my mind and body existed in a state of confusion. I felt guilty because Shawn was the one who had passed on and not me. Up until August 17, the only significant loss I'd had was my granddad. However, I knew without a doubt, just as I had with Papa, that Shawn was a Christian and had met Jesus face to face. And for that, I felt peace.

There were over 1,500 people at Shawn's funeral in his hometown of Iraan, Texas. I was a pallbearer and sitting on the stage. As the preacher was talking, suddenly, something came over me. I got up, walked over, grabbed the microphone from him, and said, "You know, this is not a sad day. I knew Shawn McMullen, and I know that he was a Christian. I know where he's at now. I know he's in heaven. He's in a way better place than where we are. I wouldn't bring him back if I could. We can't bring him back, but we can go be with him. Because of that, this is not a sad day for us."

After the funeral and graveside service, my family and I drove straight back to the ranch near Tell, which was five hours away. I had my whole family with me.

We got home about 3 a.m. We had lights in the arena and barn, and Dad turned all of them on for me. I immediately packed my trailer and got ready to leave again, and I pulled out of the driveway just as the sun was coming up. I was up at a rodeo in Bremerton, Washington, two days later, about two thousand miles away, on the northwest side of Seattle. I hadn't slept since I'd gone to bed in the trailer before the wreck—five days now—and I was on autopilot. On the drive to Bremerton, I only stopped for diesel. I think the drive was about 28 hours straight.

I really didn't know what I should do, but everybody that I came in contact with just kept saying, "You gotta do it for Shawn. You gotta go win the World Championship for Shawn. You got to keep rodeoing. You gotta keep going. You gotta do it for his family."

I didn't know anything different, so I went. I still felt numb, physically and emotionally. I don't remember what I did at Bremerton. I don't even know if I caught the calf or not.

After leaving there that night, I drove to Armstrong, British Columbia, another four or five hours away. Now, I was going on seven days with no sleep. When I pulled into Armstrong, it was dark. Suddenly, I was scared to death of the dark—and the fact that I felt so scared of the dark scared me even more.

I knew I had to sleep. I had a Capri camper on the back of my truck. I took a shower and then sat on the bed with my towel still around me to put my socks on. As I was putting one sock on, I must have fallen over because that's where I woke up the next morning. I had passed out from exhaustion. That aptly describes the rest of that year. I tried to keep rodeoing. I was physically present, but mentally, I'd checked out. I was putting on a good front for everybody, but inside... inside, I was dying.

During the rest of the year, I went to 30 rodeos and didn't win a dime at any of them. I saw my name dropping from the top ten and then out of the top 15. I didn't qualify for the NFR, and I didn't even really care.

I was in the middle of what I know now was a deep, dark depression. I was scared of everything. I felt like I was breaking apart on the inside, and I had no idea how to get away from the pain I was in. That's when I was invited again—I had been invited for years, but it had never fit my schedule—to go to a men's retreat called Walk to Emmaus.

Ironically, the retreat started the same night as the National Finals, but I decided that the retreat was where I needed to be. Maybe I didn't make it to Vegas because I was supposed to be at the Walk to Emmaus. That first night, I realized that I wasn't meant to carry my burden alone. I had taken all this pain, sorrow, guilt, and whatever else and internalized it. I had been trying to be strong for everyone around me, including myself, but I decided that night—the first night of the 1996 NFR—to lay it all down to God. I didn't need to be strong—my strength came from Christ. And God was no longer just God. He was my Father. I had been a Christian since the age of five, but that December night in 1996, I started to have a real understanding of who Father God was.

I realized I was living out Psalms 23, which says, *"Yea, though I walk through the valley of the shadow of death, I will fear no evil, for thy rod and thy staff, they comfort me."*

Well, I was able to walk through that valley, and then I did see God's goodness and mercy. That verse became a spiritual marker for me, and I would say it to myself just before roping, not as a ritual but as a reminder that the Lord is my Shepherd.

I left the Walk to Emmaus with a renewed spirit.

Change of Mission

From that point on, I started healing. I was able to remember the good times and be thankful for the time I'd had with Shawn instead of focusing on the darkness and torment of the wreck. I was so thankful for him and our friendship and for what I still had. I told myself that I'd make the most of this opportunity from here on out, not just for me, but for him and God's greater purpose in my life.

I decided I was going to enjoy both the highs and the lows. When 1997 came around, I got off to a great start, setting arena records everywhere. My career just took off from there. I was on a magical ride. It was the most blessed time of my life, and I didn't take a single moment for granted. They even put me in *People* magazine on their "Most Eligible" list, which I personally found embarrassing, seeing as how I was both extremely modest and I had fallen hard for a girl named Jennifer Douglas back in the fall of 1996.

Even in the pit of my grief, while numb to the world, her megawatt smile, kind heart, and willingness to talk to me on the phone for hours when I couldn't sleep had made me take notice. She'd caught my eye at the Cow Palace Rodeo in San Francisco, California, and it was the first time I can remember feeling anything since the wreck. I knew she was it for me.

Jennifer worked as a rodeo sideline reporter. She and I got married in 2001, and by 2003, she was pregnant with Stone, our first son. That's when my life once again turned upside down.

At the ripe old age of 32, I had a stroke.

Of course, at the time, I had no idea what was happening. Jennifer was working at a rodeo in California, and I was getting ready to practice. As I was talking to a guy working for me, all of a sudden, I couldn't speak. After I realized something was wrong, I drove myself to the emergency room. They tried asking me what was wrong, but I still couldn't make a sound, so I got a piece of paper and wrote, "I can't talk."

They ran tests, but the only thing that was wrong was that I couldn't talk. They decided I needed to go to a larger hospital, so Mom and Dad went with me to Amarillo. We got there late, nearly midnight, on a Saturday night. A guy had been shot, but he had to sit in the waiting room while they brought me right back. I started to get concerned that this could be something serious, but I didn't want anyone to tell Jennifer. No point in worrying her from across the country when the doctors didn't even know what was wrong.

The doctors ran tests on me for a couple of days before they finally determined that it was a stroke caused by a hole in my heart. A blood clot had slipped through the two chambers of my heart and hit the part of my brain that controls speech.

Jennifer was by my side when they told me there was nothing they could do to fix it. They were going to put me on a high dose of blood thinners and just hope that it didn't happen again. The doctor said, "Life as you know it is over. You'll never be able to ride a horse again. You sure can't rope. And you're going to have to change your lifestyle as far as working on the ranch and doing physical things."

I really don't remember anything he said after that.

On the way home, my speech started to come back. I looked at Jennifer and said, "Did he say what I thought he said?"

"Yeah," she replied. "You can't rope anymore."

After that, it was a pretty quiet ride home.

Change of Mission

I could live with not rodeoing, but Jennifer, a former biochemistry major, wanted to know everything there was to know about what was happening to me and if there really was nothing to be done. I just wanted to live to raise my son, but the more research that she did, the more we found out that I would probably have another stroke at some point, and the second one was usually worse. Not only that, but even a bruise could kill me. Can you imagine going through life while trying to avoid being bruised? A reckless kid with a shopping cart at the grocery store could mean my little boy was gonna grow up without a dad. So, Jennifer started calling different places that specialized in treating my heart condition, patent foramen ovale, better known as a PFO—or, in cowboy terms, a hole in your heart.

We found three places in the United States that were doing experimental surgery to close the hole. Basically, they put a patch on it like you would patch a tire. Dr. Tandy Freeman, the sports medicine doctor in Dallas who has performed at least five surgeries on me, found Dr. Carey Kimmelstiel, a cardiologist, and Dr. David Thaler, a neurologist, at the New England Medical Center in Boston, who worked hand in hand. We reached out to them, and that's when we found out that the surgery was not FDA-approved, which meant the doctors could not do it without special approval.

Once the FDA approved the experimental surgery, we were on a plane. My whole family, Jennifer and my mom, my dad, and my three sisters, all flew to Boston for this surgery. My room was a revolving door of PAs, nurses, and other hospital staff. They wanted to see this 32-year-old cowboy stroke guy— I felt like a science experiment.

The night before the surgery, we were in a hotel room, and I knew I had to have this talk with Jennifer, who was five months pregnant with our first son. I was so excited to be a dad. I absolutely adored kids. I loved playing any kind of sport or game, teaching roping lessons, and playing football with them. Being the youngest in my family by quite a few years, with three older sisters, I had a lot of experience with my nieces and nephews. I had waited to be where I could really enjoy my own kids before we had our own, and there was nothing I was looking forward to more at that point in my life than being a dad.

So, I thought, "I've got to have this conversation with her." I found myself in the shower, on my hands and knees, talking it over with the Lord and saying, "You've got to give me the words to say to her." I knew I needed to explain to her the story in John 11:4, where Jesus, talking about Lazarus, says, *"This sickness won't end in death but for the glory of my Father."* I remember reading that and thinking, *Those are my words. Those words weren't just written for Lazarus. They were written for me, too.*

I got out of the shower, went to her, and said, "I have to talk to you before the surgery tomorrow. If something happens on that operating table and I don't make it through, know this: That's what's going to be best for you and our little boy, and what is best for y'all is what I want. If this does end up in my death, which I don't believe it is, I'm standing on John 11. As it says in Romans 8:28, *'God works in all things for those who love him who've been called according to his purpose.'* I know God will work in this, too." That's probably the hardest conversation I've ever had with her, but I truly meant every word.

The day for the surgery came. I had already had a handful of surgeries, just enough to make me think that I knew what to expect. This time, though, if there were complications, they would have to cut my chest open. So, using cowboy logic, I said to myself, *I need to put this gown on with the opening in front so that it'll be easy for them to get to me, right?* So, I put it on that way before the surgery, and they wheeled me into the operating room.

As I was lying there, this nurse walked up and said, "Oh, honey, you've got your gown on backwards."

"No, ma'am, I don't," I replied.

"Yeah, you do. It's supposed to open in the back."

And I said, "Well, if you've got to open my chest if things go bad…"

"Oh, no, no, no. They have a way of getting right to you, but you gotta put it on the right way with the opening in the back."

It was then that my ears started to burn because I knew what this meant. I am extremely, awkwardly modest, but this nurse made me stand up and take off my gown, and then she put it back on me the right way as I stood there in all my glory—and as cold as that operating room was, there wasn't a whole lot of glory! I thought, *Man, I didn't know heart surgery was going to be this tough.*

The next thing I remember, I was waking up in the recovery room, and the first thing I did was feel my chest. The same nurse was there, and she said to me, "Oh, honey, everything went fine."

Thankfully, as the doctor said when I saw him, "Everything was textbook." They went in through my artery and put in a device called an Abbott Amplatzer, kind of like a patch on a tire that sealed off the two chambers of my heart.

We came home, and I spent about two months in recovery. I felt good, but we still didn't know for sure if the doctors were going to clear me to rodeo again. At that time, a horse that I had wanted to buy my whole career came up for sale. One of my best friends, Trent Walls, owned him, and he called me and said, "Stran, you want to buy Topper?"

"Trent," I said, "I would love to."

Now, the thing about Topper was that he was probably the greatest calf-roping horse there ever was, but he was 21 years old. In human years, that would be equal to his mid to late 70s. The prime of his athletic life was gone. And Trent wanted an extremely large amount of money for this horse. I talked it over with Jennifer, and then I discussed it with my parents and a few other people. Except for Jennifer, everybody pretty much thought that I was the craziest person in the world for wanting to buy a 21-year-old horse for that amount of money, not knowing if I was going to be able to rope again or not.

However, Jen said, "You've always wanted this horse, so go buy him." So, go buy him, I did.

Now, I kind of missed a spot here.

In the middle of all this, my best horse, Whoa, also had a stroke. I was in the hospital, and Jennifer had to decide with the veterinarian to put him down because the stroke had hit the part of his brain controlling his equilibrium, and he couldn't even stand. I always said it was a sympathy stroke. I knew that if I was ever cleared to rope again, I was going to need a horse, so I decided to buy this old, used-up horse that was my dream horse.

I went and picked Topper up before I was even cleared to start roping again. I spent the day with my friend Trent. He'd rodeoed with me since I was in college, and he just knew that this horse and I were made for each other.

As I was driving home with Topper, I stopped at a roadside park just south of Guthrie, Texas, out in the middle of nowhere. I unloaded him from the trailer and walked him around. It was like I was a kid on Christmas Day. With no one else around, I stood there, looking at him, and then I started crying. I couldn't believe it.

So, I started praying. I said, "Lord, you know you made this possible, and I know that I've heard from you about this, and I don't want to miss this. This horse is not mine. I'm giving him to you. Anything that comes out of this, the story that you are able to tell out of this with him, is going to be your story, not mine. He's your horse. He's not mine."

Change of Mission

I put him back in the trailer and drove home, and about six weeks later, they cleared me to start roping. The first rodeo I went to on Topper, I won the short round. It was like Michael Jordan had finally found Scottie Pippin. I felt ten feet tall and bulletproof. It was amazing what I was able to accomplish with him and how I felt.

Topper helped me qualify for the 2004 NFR, and I not only qualified, but I had a chance to finally win a World Championship. At the NFR, it came down to the tenth go-round. Even though I was able to win it, it wasn't quite enough. I missed winning the gold buckle by less than $1,500.

Check out Stran's 2004 10th Go-Round run. Scan the QR Code:

Bonus Video Content!

In rodeoing, like any other sport, your goal is to be the world champion. You don't really remember who the runner-up was. There are no silver buckles for second place. I was so close. So close. What hurt so badly was getting so close after everything that I'd just overcome. Twenty-one months earlier, I'd been told I would never swing a rope or throw a leg over a horse again. My best friend died, my horse died, and I nearly died, but here I was, less than two years later, primed to be a world champion. And I missed it by the smallest of margins. It was a heartbreaker, but as they say in rodeo, it was on to the next one.

In 2005, to save Topper, I decided to be pretty selective about where I went. Great horses are like great cars… they only have so many miles they can go, so I was very strategic about where we entered. I rode him at less than 30 rodeos and won over $90,000, which was almost unheard of. Topper was named the AQHA/PRCA Horse of the Year that year, which is still one of my proudest moments in rodeo—not for myself, but for him. If I had never owned Topper, I would still say that. He was, in my opinion, one of the greatest calf horses of all time. In 2005, Jen and I welcomed our second son, Scout. Between being selective about my rodeos with Topper and staying closer to home for my family, my goal was to just make the Finals again, which I did.

The next year was a struggle. Topper was older, of course, 24 years at that point, which calculates to about 84 in human years, so I really was trying to take care of him and not use him very much. I only rode him at the very best rodeos, even less than the year before. I was in an unfamiliar spot—just outside of the top 15—and it came down to the last week of the rodeo season. It was going to take a lot of miles if I wanted to make the NFR. I decided to ride another horse to save Topper for the Finals, and at the very last rodeo of the season, I had to win third to qualify. I put everything on the line, even if it meant sacrificing my body to get the job done.

Unfortunately, I injured my right arm during the run. I finished, but as I rode out, I knew it was bad. I didn't know it at the time, but in the middle of the run, I had dislocated my shoulder and torn all the ligaments away from the bone. I should not have been able to complete the run, but I did. Of course, I wasn't fast enough to be able to finish in the top three.

I rode out of the arena feeling completely numb. I could tell that my right arm was out of the socket because it was about three to four inches lower than my left. I couldn't move it at all, and when they announced my time, I instantly knew my 2006 NFR quest was not going to happen. A whole year down the drain, a whole year of struggle, with the worst ending I could imagine.

I knew that this was the worst injury I'd ever had. Not only was my shoulder dislocated, but it sounded like gears grinding when I moved the wrong way. I found out later that my arm was being held on my body by skin only. I rode right by the Justin Sports Medicine people, who could see that something was wrong with me, and out of the arena. I rode all the way out to the parking lot where my truck and trailer were. As I rode up to the rig, I was crying.

I was devastated, but not about losing a chance at winning the glory of a World Championship or anything like that. When you rodeo professionally, you pay your own entry fees, fuel, vet expenses, travel, etc. It is extremely expensive to go down the road full-time and keep both you and your horses in top physical shape. It's all a gamble. The only way you can stay in the black is by making it to the NFR. So, trying to figure out how I was going to provide for my wife and two babies at home was a big part of the devastation I felt. Plus, when I looked down at my right arm, which was what my whole career hinged on, I could tell that the injury was very bad.

Despite my tears and fears, for some reason, a peace came over me. I lifted my left hand and said, "Thank you, Lord, for this. Thank you in advance. I can't wait to see what you're going to do because I know you didn't bring me this far just to bring me this far. I know this is bad, and you say you work in all things. Well, I'm excited to see what you are going to do here."

Then I got off my horse, unsaddled him with my left arm, and pointed the truck south.

It took 14 hours to get home in Childress, Texas. When I returned, Jen and I immediately went to see Dr. Tandy Freeman, the orthopedic surgeon in Dallas. After taking an MRI, he confirmed what I already knew: this was bad, probably career-ending, but we scheduled surgery anyway.

After the surgery, he came out to talk to Jennifer. He told her that if I were a pitcher, my career would be over due to the loss of the range of motion of my right arm. But he thought I could teach myself to rope again.

Jennifer said, "Well, isn't it somewhat the same range of motion that he needs to be able to rope?"

"Well, yeah," he said, "and if he played a team sport, I would not be able to clear him."

"But it's the same, right?" she asked.

"Maybe he can teach himself to rope a different way," he replied.

Basically, that was like saying that my career was over. The range of motion that I needed would never return.

This was in November, and the National Finals are in December. So, a month later, Jennifer was working for ESPN and doing the telecast out there, and I went with her. The last place I wanted to be was at the National Finals because, number one, I'm not much of a spectator, and number two, my arm was in this pillow sling, and I was still in a ton of pain. Everybody I saw asked, "Oh, my gosh. How did that happen? How are you? When are you gonna be able to rope again?" I tried to smile and give them the best answers I could, but the truth was, I didn't even know myself. The answer might be never.

The PRCA had a dinner one night, and they invited Jennifer and me to go with them. This was the last thing I wanted to do, but she had supported me through the worst times of my life, so the least I could do was put on a smile and go along with her. The ProRodeo Commissioner, CEO of Wrangler, and several other dignitaries were there, including a televangelist named Paula White. We started talking with Paula, and she learned our story. At the time, she was the chaplain of the New York Yankees and was used to being around big-time professional athletes. I'm still not quite sure what she saw in a grumpy cowboy from Texas with a pillow under his arm. For some reason, she felt led to connect me with her trainer.

Now, her trainer wasn't your run-of-the-mill guy at the gym. Dodd Romero was literally the trainer to the stars. His client list included Denzel Washington, Alex Rodriguez, Lenny Kravitz, Charlize Theron, and Jennifer Lopez, to name a few. He seemed untouchable for us. Paula said, "I just feel like I'm supposed to share his contact with you and get you two connected."

I had no idea how this chain of events was going to impact not just my career but my family and life. He would change how I approach every day. I had the work ethic, and I was already extremely disciplined. But Dodd would help me put an intentional process into my practice. I learned how to apply the self-discipline that kept me going on all-night drives and practicing in the pen for hours after I should have quit, to habits like proper sleep, clean eating, and going to the gym instead of running 20 more calves. I learned the practice of quality runs over quantity runs. I couldn't believe that this chance meeting with Paula White might lead to a cowboy like me getting to train with a guy like Dodd Romero. The chances of that were about as good as me getting to meet and write a book with Colonel Craig Flowers. But it wasn't chance at all—it had to be a God thing.

We flew to San Antonio and met Dodd for the first time in a hotel lobby. My first thought when I saw him was, *Oh, my lord, I hope this man doesn't break me in half.* He looked like the Incredible Hulk. Then I thought, *We have absolutely zero in common.* He was wearing huge, baggy sweats and looked to weigh about 250 or 260. His muscles looked like skin pulled over chiseled rock. He was 3%, maybe 4%, body fat and had dreads that hung halfway down his back. He didn't speak English. "He speaks in Greek warrior," I always say. For instance, if you're going to eat breakfast, in a deep voice like none other, he will say, "My brother, in the morning, before we prepare for battle, we will replenish the body with the nutrients that are required for us to complete our mission on this day." In cowboy terms, that means: "We're going to go eat breakfast."

I was so intimidated by him and thought, *There's no way this is going to work.* But after five minutes with him, I knew we had a special connection. We visited for probably three or four hours in this hotel lobby, and I realized who this man was. We had one thing in common. Yeah, we definitely had one thing in common. We both loved the Lord, and he was my brother—and he considered me a God-appointed assignment.

After hours of visiting, and getting to know each other, he said, "I never take an assignment that I don't feel like is from God." Then he added, "My brother, I'm not only going to train you; I'm going to completely transform you physically. You're going to be better. You're going to be faster. You're going to be stronger. You're going to be lighter. You're going to do what you've never done before, in and out of the arena. I promise it. We're going to get you a gold buckle."

Meanwhile, I was thinking, *Just get me where I can get my arm up over my head. I know how to do everything else. Just get me where I can swing a rope again.*

"I will call you when it's time," he said.

Once again, Change of Mission.

Scan the QR code for bonus video content.

Bonus Video Content!

CHAPTER 2

Great to Elite: The 4%

"I have noticed over several decades that the Elite have a lot in common. They remain situationally aware and self-aware and then do what 96% of us do not: they take action."
–J. Craig Flowers

• • •

BLUF: Situational Awareness, Self-Awareness, and the courage (heart) to Act is a competitive edge.

• • •

Jim Collins wrote a wonderful book entitled *Good to Great*. I suspect many of our readers have that book and have referred to it many times. It's a remarkable work, and I appreciate it very much. What we'll break down a little bit more in this chapter is *great to elite*.

In 2012, I had the privilege of flying to Louisiana on a private plane after I'd retired from the Army. We were on an "organic protein harvest" (we were duck hunting!). On board were some of the most successful men in business, specifically construction, oil and gas, and insurance. I sat quietly and listened to how they communicated, what they talked about, what their priorities of work (POW) were, and how they continued to develop themselves. They discussed how they responded to success, failure, and setbacks. Part of the discussion was on how the elite find and support one another on their journey to becoming elite.

They spoke about an article that they had read that said that the elite only comprise 4% of the population, whether it's in business, sports, or any other endeavor. I wish I could cite the article they were discussing. I simply don't know what it was. They showed it to me briefly. I was the new guy and didn't want to disrupt the flow of the conversation. This was before smartphones; otherwise, I would have snapped a photo of it. I do recall clearly, however, that only 4% have the elite *behaviors* (not talent) that allow them to win in business, education, sports, and life.

Theodore Roosevelt said, "Far better it is to dare mighty things, to win glorious triumphs, even though checkered by failure, than to take rank with those poor spirits who neither enjoy much nor suffer much, because they live in the gray twilight that knows neither victory nor defeat." In preparation for writing this book, I spent time with some elite special operators. These are the "dudes" teenagers and others often pretend to be when they play *Call of Duty*, *Fortnite*, and *Rainbow 6 Siege* video games.

Let's take the Green Berets, a branch of the United States Army. They fall under the umbrella of the special operations community. I was not a Green Beret. However, I had the rare privilege of serving in a direct support role to elite special operators, including the Green Berets, Navy SEALs, and others. Others are often referred to as special mission units or SMUs.

All members of this *community* have a very unique way of behaving. One trait is a change-of-mission mindset: The moment something fundamentally new occurs during a mission or operation, they change their mindset, their focus. I'm not talking about a small event or a speed bump along the way. I mean a significant event like Stran went through. I can't say exactly when it occurs, but it happens quickly and without emotion, and every member of the team involved accepts the new conditions and direction of the mission.

In businesses I've worked with over the last 15 years, I've noticed a lack of situational awareness along with a stubborn refusal to make adjustments when faced with the unexpected. Something disrupts the business plan (COVID, for example), and the named leaders either freeze, throw their hands up in the air, or shut down. The same thing occurs in big government and politics. Bureaucrats simply give up or just try to get through the day without accomplishing much at all. They repeat this until *their* "normal" returns. Often, it never does. It's why our government continues to grow out of hand. We just keep hiring more people who don't do much, especially during difficult, uncertain times.

Not the elite. The elite train for chaos. They train the behaviors required to win during chaotic times. They don't look for trouble, but they're never surprised when it comes their way. They roll with the chaos and find new ways to adapt, create, and innovate. Even the most disciplined person, like Stran Smith, if they haven't trained in the behaviors required for chaotic times, they often only know one thing to do: Work harder. That's not a mission, mindset, or process. Hard work is required, but it's not enough to consistently win and accomplish the mission.

THE PREFRONTAL CORTEX

I'm familiar with Stran's story. The truth is, as close as he got to winning the World Championship in his 20s, it wasn't his time to win the gold buckle. It *could* have happened if it hadn't been for all the significant setbacks that occurred along the way. As many variables as there are in rodeo, and there are thousands, the battles Stran fought were like nothing you could ever prepare for. After the accident happened and Shawn passed away, Stran did have a mission. However, he had the wrong mindset and his only process was to work harder and sacrifice his body with every run. Stran's prefrontal cortex, which is responsible for decision-making and emotions, was not fully prepared to win. His body may have been—the physical talent was there—but his brain was not ready.

Now, one could not have convinced Stran of this. At 25, he was driven by emotion and tragedy; he was like a madman chasing a ghost. He lacked, believe it or not, a disciplined plan. Yes, Stran Smith, one of the most disciplined men I have ever known, was undisciplined. Because of the significant emotional events he endured, sometimes called the crucibles of life, it was very unlikely that he would have won. Had I told him that in his mid to late 20s, he would have disregarded that advice. Thankfully, we didn't meet until well after those years.

So, let's return to the Green Berets. One of my best friends is a retired Green Beret with 11 combat deployments. I work out with him almost every morning. To confirm what I already believed, I asked him, "What are the average ages of an A-team leader and its members?"

Some may remember the TV show *The A-Team* with Mr. T. There truly is an A-Team, and it is the first team that an Army Green Beret officer has the privilege of leading. An A-Team consists of 12 Green Berets. The average A-Team member is… in their 30s. Rarely is anyone under 25.

Our nation's security is at stake, so these teams *must* win against our enemies. There is no room for an underdeveloped prefrontal cortex. And by the way, in case you ever wondered, no other nation on the planet comes even close to having a special operations community like ours. They are the best in the world, but the average age of a Green Beret Alpha team member is the early 30s. In fact, at least two of the members are in their 40s. They cannot afford to have an underdeveloped prefrontal cortex, which, for men, doesn't fully develop until around 26 or 27 years old (as late as 29 for some). For women, and I am the father of three daughters, it will develop earlier, as early as 23, but likely around 24 or 25. For men, well, we have the privilege of a couple more years to develop decision-making skills and manage our emotions.

TRUSTING THE PROCESS

When Stran started his journey of becoming a world champion, he was 25 years old. When you go back and read that story again—and I think we can all agree that there has to be a documentary or a movie made about it—think about what he was trying to do without having fully developed his mind and without any process.

Nick Saban, the former head coach at the University of Alabama, whom I've met on three occasions, is famous for saying, "Trust the process." In fact, he's so famous for saying it that leaders in industry, education, and sports repeat the phrase without knowing what the heck it means. Stran Smith did not have a process at the age of 25. You see, *working hard and* going without sleep, for example, is not a process.

Working hard is expected, a requirement. It's not a choice. It's certainly a requirement of the elite, but working hard is just a small PART of a bigger *process*. The Green Berets are mature men of character, integrity, and talent who are driven by real processes.

The Green Berets have forced sleep plans as part of their process. They build rest, recovery, hydration, etc., into their planning and execution. They know that rest, recovery, and nutrition are all part of the process that allows them to accomplish their mission. However, I promise you if I had met Stran Smith at 25 and told him he needed to get six to eight hours of sleep, driven by ego and emotion, he may have laughed at my suggestion. He would have continued on those long journeys to the next rodeo because he was driven by emotion. He wanted to win the World Championships because of Shawn.

It wasn't a process; it was simply naïve, hard work driven by a significant emotional event that included death, injury, and continuous setbacks, the kind that are unimaginable for most. His reaction to that was very emotional and typical. In fact, it's how most of us behave when we have a significant emotional event, but not the elite.

The elite, who have fully developed prefrontal cortexes, put in place real processes that are devoid of emotion so they can quickly and objectively sort through what I often call distractions that take away from what truly is their priority of work (POW). The average person focuses so much on their path, plan, and wants that when new information is introduced (good or bad), such as tragedy or death, they do not have a plan. They fail to adapt, and chaos is allowed to drive erratic, unreasonable behavior. They do not have a process to handle the new information. Their mission remains the same, and they fail.

RUTS OF LIFE

In preparation for an assignment abroad, my wife and I both went through a special two-day driver training on a race track in West Virginia. The instructors were incredible, true professionals. It's also why I will never buy a car that was once a "rental." For two days, we learned reverse J-turns, forward J-turns, where and how to crash into a vehicle barricade, and other maneuvers you may see in films. For many reasons, the instructors would not allow both the husband and wife to be in the same car during the training (which I thought was hilarious). Miss Beth was in her car, and I was in mine—we didn't see each other after the morning safety briefings.

One morning, the instructor talked about avoiding distractions. He asked if all of us remembered, as boys and girls, riding a bicycle and having the front tire get caught between the sidewalk and grass (i.e., a "rut"). He said, "No matter how hard you tried, you'll remember the tire would not come out of the rut. The reason your tire stayed in the rut was because you were staring at the rut. If you want to get out of the rut, look toward the place you want to go, and you will naturally go there."

I've found this analogy to be true in life. No matter the circumstance, we are doomed to stay in a rut until it comes to a natural end (the end of the sidewalk), or we can choose to understand that the rut is a temporary distraction. If we just look toward where we want to go and NOT at the rut, our energy and focus will take us in that direction. Think about that the next time you tell yourself while driving, *Don't hit the pothole, don't hit the pothole. BAM! I hit the pothole.* Why? You were looking at the pothole. Look where you want to go, not where you may be currently stuck.

LEADERSHIP LABORATORIES

Without knowing it, Stran went through crucibles and leadership laboratories of life that were developing him for what would turn out years later to be a gold buckle win. A leadership laboratory is any arena in life where we have the opportunity to practice or rep elite service to one of life's six causes. Often, the leader lab is the result of a major event in life where we have the opportunity to grow and develop, but not the guarantee. Recognizing and seizing upon the opportunity is rare. Sometimes, life forces us to develop. Other times, it is a choice. For the elite, however, it is a requirement. It really was not until Stran was literally helpless and could not lift his arm that he accepted a mission, mindset, and process-driven path to win.

We are born with a personality, but our character is developed. Character is developed by choice, circumstance, or training. Rest assured, it's developed. Character is developed through our thoughts and practice: #CharacterReps. For example, many of us have pets. In fact, we had a wonderful dog that was with us for 12 years when we were stationed in Morocco. Her name was Dolly. She had a great personality, a black and white English spaniel. *"She was a proper dog"* (you should have read that with an English accent, btw).

If I were to ask you, "Tell me about your pet," you might say, "Oh, we love our pet. You know, we *didn't* choose our pet. Our pet chose us. We went to the rescue, and without question, we knew right away that they were our pet." Why? How did you know? Because of its personality, perhaps. Maybe it was the runt of the litter or had a quiet demeanor or lots of energy. For whatever reason, most people choose their pets because of their personality. But if the character is not developed in that pet, though they might have a great personality, they're going to crap all over the house.

Stran was born with a competitive, curious, energetic, and stubborn personality. Yes, he was raised by a mother and father who encouraged him, taught him the difference between right and wrong, and made him do things like sweep the porch each day. Those character reps, coupled with his personality, drove him to work hard. However, as we know, working hard is not a process. We can work really, really hard (waste a lot of time) just to feel like we're committed to a task and still not accomplish our mission. Fatigue crumbles all. Without a process, we often cannot and will not focus on what we should do. There was no way Stran was going to be among the 4% without a process. He needed to go through crucibles of life that would develop his prefrontal cortex like no other. They would force him to manage his emotions and decision-making.

LEADERSHIP: SERVICE TO A CAUSE

In my career, I've learned from some great leaders, some of whom have PhDs and are now close friends. One of them is Dr. Octavious Bishop, aka "The Big O." He played football for the University of Texas as an offensive lineman. In fact, he was the left tackle who blocked for Heisman Trophy winner Ricky Williams. Dr. Octavious Bishop taught me a lot about the brain, the development of the prefrontal cortex, and how important it is, especially for people under 25, when it comes to having extraordinary situational and self-awareness and then taking action. Stran only took action. He thought working hard was a process. It was not. Stran's situational and self-awareness had yet to be developed.

Another great PhD I learned from was Colonel Eric Kail. I had the privilege of serving with him on the banks of the mighty Hudson River at a place called West Point, the birthplace of leadership for our nation, founded in 1802. He passed away shortly after we both retired from the Army. I think of him nearly every day. Eric worked in the Department of Behavioral Science and Leadership, one of 13 academic departments.

From 2004 to 2005, I served as the assistant baseball coach for West Point. It was a remarkable year, as we got our first win in the NCAA College Baseball Tournament (I'm required by law to write *for the first time in history*); we also swept Navy in four games :). During this time, COL Kail and I talked a lot about how to best reach, teach, and develop athletes to maximize their talent. The three-star general and West Point superintendent reminded ALL new instructors and professors during onboarding that leadership was our focus. Lieutenant General Bill Lennox said, "I know you have specific academic specialties and syllabuses that will drive your daily instruction. I want all of you to know, however, that *our mission is to develop leaders of character—ultimately, we are all here to teach leadership.*"

Eric and I agreed. In its simplest form, leadership is nothing more than "service." I lengthened it to "service to cause." That's it. If we're serving a cause, we're leading. When we define leadership simply, we empower everyone: the introvert, the newest member of the team, and even those who may be thinking of going somewhere else (employee retention). It's up to the named leader, however, to define leadership for the team.

Countless books have been written on leadership. You can't swing a book about leadership in an airport without hitting another book about leadership. However, I've never seen the term written in such simple terms: Leadership = Service to a Cause.

My personal, full definition of leadership is that it is "authentic, relentless, and selfless service to a cause." Use it if you would like. Essentially, we have six causes in our lives. I've given this a lot of thought and spoken about it across the country. These six causes are faith, family, friends, community, teams, and self.

The blind spot for most is self. It's not selfish to serve ourselves. In fact, for some of the most elite in the world, whom I've had the privilege of serving, it's a requirement. They serve themselves every day. Sleep, for example. They make sure that they get at least four hours. A sleep plan is part of their operations. There are some great YouTubers and podcasters I follow who claim they hate sleep. It's true for them. However, recovery, rest, and healing are part of the process. I hated sleeping for a while because I loved one particular job I had at West Point. I could not wait to get up in the morning and do more. I knew, however, that if I wanted to truly be authentic, relentless, and selfless, I needed a process that included a rest plan.

EASY WINS

After resting, the elite get early and immediate wins. Even before they *make their beds,* they earn a win. They get their first win of the day by doing the simplest of things: *not hitting snooze.* Try this simple act for a week and watch how it impacts you. Decide what time you're getting up the night prior and answer the *call to serve* for five straight mornings. You'll start your day 1-0 without leaving your bedside. For one week, DON'T HIT SNOOZE.

The elite commit to a needed period of rest and recovery, something Stran did not do. He refused to rest and recover to accomplish his mission. The elite make rest a part of their process. They may hate resting, but so what? Their feelings don't matter. They stick to their process, and by doing so, they are serving/leading themselves AND serving their team by remaining in an optimal state of readiness.

In football, the analogy would be that the ball is snapped, the play is started, and they put their feet on the ground. The average person, after hitting the snooze button two or three times, might think, *Good Lord, it's morning,* and they might even say it out loud. But not the elite.

The elite, no matter how tired they are, put their feet on the ground. There's something about putting one's feet on the ground. Try it. Just sling your feet over the side of the bed and let them touch the ground. You may lay there for a few moments, but in just a few short moments, you will sit up. And instead of saying, "Oh, Lord, it's morning," Stran says, "Good morning, Lord." That is a very different way to answer the bell—a great way to start 1-0.

THE HIJACKED AMYGDALA

Another vital part of the brain to be aware of is the amygdala. I knew nothing about the amygdala, that acorn-sized part of your brain that sits just behind your brain stem, until I learned about it from Dr. Jat Thompson. The CEO and founder of Horizon Performance, Jat earned his PhD at North Carolina State—coincidently, his classmate was Colonel Eric Kail. Horizon Performance works with some of the most elite teams in the world in athletics, our military, and business. If you have the opportunity to work with Horizon Performance, do it. In fact, Horizon Performance, based in North Carolina, had a hand in helping select astronauts for the Mars mission. For Horizon, performance is not about talent. Yes, you have to have enough talent to be on the board, but really, it's about the behaviors and the processes required to become elite.

While I was working with an NCAA athletics department in the Southeastern Conference, Dr. Thompson and I discussed the amygdala. Honestly, he did most of the talking; I listened. The term in behavioral science is "amygdala hijack," and it is a threat to all of us.

The amygdala is the part of the brain that's responsible for the fight-or-flight response. I call it my fourth daughter, as it's spelled "Amy G. Dala." This is how Dr. Thompson explained the "stack" to me: Imagine that your smartphone died last night. The battery simply quit, so the alarm did not go off, and you woke up late; that's stack number one. You take one or two steps and stub your toe; that's stack number two. You're running late and hurrying around the corner, and because you haven't developed character in your new puppy, he's made a mess. You step in it; that's another stack. You get in for your first cup of coffee, and as you reach for the mug, you knock it over; that's stack number four. Everybody is different, but eventually, you hit the "stack," the straw that breaks the camel's back, and your amygdala gets hijacked.

For most of us, once our amygdala is hijacked—and Stran Smith's amygdala was certainly hijacked—we strike out with emotion. In some of the worst cases, we may snap at somebody that we need or love in our lives. For example, we can't find our car keys as we're heading out the door, and the car that we intended to fill up the night before is sitting empty. And then a spouse or child innocently comes in and asks: "Has anyone seen my shoes?" or "Has anyone seen my book bag?" Because our amygdala has been hijacked, we turn on them with emotion and say something that, about 20 minutes later, we're going to regret.

This does not happen to the elite. They train in environments that *force* stacking. The Green Berets, for example, routinely put themselves in training environments where they must manage their emotions and decisions based on new information and then immediately take action. They also allow their teammates to tell them when they are "stacking," and they train situational and self-awareness.

I speak French, which is not handy in the great state of Texas. The French word for heart is *coeur*. That happens to be the root word of *cour*age. The Green Berets have the courage to act not because they were born with it as a part of their personality but because they developed and trained it. However, this only occurred after their prefrontal cortex was fully developed, somewhere around the age of 26 or 27, driven by training situations.

In Stran's case, his prefrontal cortex was driven by significant emotional events. Coupled with his personality, his prefrontal cortex developed like an elite special operator, but not until he was in his 30s. It'll take some discipline for the reader not to skip ahead to read the last chapter here on how Stran's story eventually ended in Las Vegas.

But stay with us because Stran and I, who've known each other for a decade or so, have leaned on one another to continue our personal development. We have tried, as often as we've been called upon, to *educate, train, and inspire* those who have asked us to work with their organizations.

Part of West Point's mission statement is to *educate, train, and inspire.* Many will claim they want to be among the 4%. If I were to ambush you right now and say, "Would you like to become elite?" of course, you would say yes.

If I asked you if you wanted to be great, of course, you would say yes. And if I asked you if you wanted to be average, you would say, "No, I don't want to be average. I wouldn't be reading this book if I wanted to be average."

Well, are you willing to commit to a real process and not just work hard, which is expected? Are you willing to ensure that your prefrontal cortex is fully developed and that you are able to manage your amygdala? Many of you right now are reflecting on exactly when your amygdala was last hijacked. Some are smiling right now, saying, "It happened to me today," either at work or at home, or on a team, or perhaps at church. It happens to most of us every single day.

WHAT IT TAKES TO BE ELITE

We're going to explore the process of how the elite train and how they think and act in a way that allows them to win consistently. Once you are a part of an elite team, you do NOT want to leave. I knew senior SEALs in their 40s who turned down promotions, more money, and more opportunities for prestige and rank so that they could stay with their team. They did this because they wanted to be part of an elite team, which is rare. Think about it: 96% are not elite.

Jim Collins talks about going from *Good to Great,* and I love his book and recommend it. Here, though, we're talking about the rare, exceptional 4%. That's different. That takes different behavior. That takes a different level of discipline. It is trainable. That's the good news. Even in one's 20s, it's trainable. But it's also developed through significant emotional events like Stran Smith went through, such as loss, setbacks, injuries, more loss, and more setbacks.

Mission, mindset, process. The United States has the world's most elite units, able to handle any mission they may be given. Because of them, we rest well, perhaps even naively, here at home. As George Orwell wrote, "We sleep silently in our beds because rough men stand ready in the night to visit violence on those who would do us harm."

Scan the code for bonus video content!

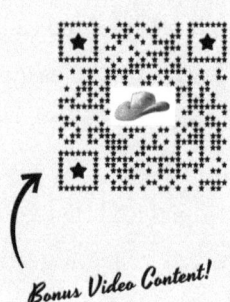

Bonus Video Content!

CHAPTER 3

How the Most Elite in the World Train and Behave to Win

"I never expected to arrive. And that's how I stayed hungry."
−Stran Smith

• • •

BLUF: The elite fully commit to preparing. They do this objectively and consistently, without emotion, driven by a mission, mindset, and process.

• • •

When I was around 11 or 12 years old, I told my mother I wanted an alarm clock. She bought me one that talked when it would go off. I can still remember what it said: Beep, "The time is 5:30 a.m. It's time to wake up," beep. I started playing a game with myself when I had to get up extremely early because we lived 20 miles from school, and I caught the bus at 6:10 a.m., which meant I had to wake up at about 5:30. So I made a game of it. I put the alarm clock across the room, where I couldn't hit the snooze, and when the alarm first beeped, I tried to turn it off before it said the time.

I had no idea what I was doing back then, but it's something that has stuck with me to this day. Whenever I hear the Colonel say, "Don't hit the snooze," I think, "I haven't been hitting the snooze for about 45 years now."

Without realizing it, Stran Smith created a leadership laboratory that developed his prefrontal cortex. Can you imagine making that decision at 12 years old? Normally, most kids that age have to get their little legs rubbed by mom, dad, or some other family member to get out of bed.

Little did Stran know that by doing this, he was setting himself up to be on the world stage in 2008. The first thing the elite do is admit to themselves that their intentions simply do not matter. You either hit the snooze button this morning, or you did not. You exercised today, or you did not. You either wrote that thank-you note, made the sales call, or went to the meeting on time, or you did not. You either spent time with the newest member of your team, business, or company, or you did not. You either apologized for something you said or did or... you did not.

You edited the text before you sent it, or you did not. Same thing with an email. Most of us edit our emails and texts after we send them, but not the elite. They have extraordinary situational and self-awareness and then the courage, the heart, to act.

My family and I were stationed in The Kingdom of Morocco for three years. Military members living overseas don't have the luxury of watching regular American television. Our only TV channel was the Armed Forces Network (AFN), on which we would watch reruns of *I Dream of Jeannie*, *Gilligan's Island*, and *Seinfeld*. The ads during the breaks were not like the ones you typically see, like an insurance or beer commercial. (Incidentally, there's a reason why insurance companies have higher costs for males who are 25 years and younger. They know their prefrontal cortexes are not yet fully developed.)

Instead of regular advertising, the AFN pipelines messaging from the Pentagon. Some of these messages are very corny, sometimes entertaining and informative. One segment featured two soldiers sitting at a bar and enjoying their beverages. Now, whether you're in the Army, Air Force, Navy, Marines, or Coast Guard, you are required to take a biannual physical fitness test. Most officers wanted the maximum physical fitness score, which was 300 points. (I know it's changed since I retired, but back when I served on active duty, it was 300 points.) That was hard to do. To get that score, you had to do exercise outside the daily routines. You had to do extra.

Now, in this ad, one of the soldiers says to the other, "Next week, we have our annual physical fitness test. Let's meet at the track tomorrow and begin training for it." Keep in mind that a soldier must pass the test to remain on active duty. In this case, they've given themselves a week to prepare. The second soldier looks at the first and says, "I'll see you at the track in the morning," and then they raise their beverages and toast to meeting at the track.

In the next scene, they're at the track. After running around one time (400 meters), they rather dramatically fall into the grass-covered infield, huffing and puffing. As they're lying there, another soldier runs around effortlessly, clearly not winded (perhaps he had trained with someone like Dodd Romero). One of the soldiers on the infield looks at the other and says, "Wow, look at that guy. How does he do it?"

"I don't know," his companion replies, "but he's out here *every day*."

The elite just don't do it every now and then. They do it every single day.

Now, I'm not saying that on a Sunday or a day off, the elite don't occasionally sleep in. However, I've been around them, and even on days off, they have a hard time not waking up early because they've trained themselves so well.

SITUATIONAL AWARENESS, SELF-AWARENESS, AND TAKING ACTION

I was concerned that my family would be living abroad for many years, and I wanted our daughters to have extraordinary situational and self-awareness and the courage to act. I needed to create a leadership lab for them.

I used the shopping mall as a leadership laboratory to train their prefrontal cortexes and make them aware of the X. Being on the X is not a good thing. When one is "on the X," one has two choices: fight or flight. And yes, "Amy G. Dala" plays a part. When I work with college quarterbacks, I tell them, "When you are in the pocket, you have a limited amount of time. You are on the X, and the defensive end is coming. Get off the X, or prepare to fight against getting sacked."

I would get the girls all fired up on the day that we were going to spend together, saying that we were going to go get ice cream or a cookie or pick out a new dress or some new shoes. Then I would load all three girls up, and we would go to the nearby shopping mall and park rather far away from the entrance. I held the hands of the two youngest girls while the oldest girl skipped alongside, and before we got to the entrance, I would say, "Girls, let's pause for a moment and sit down on this bench."

Once we were all sitting, I'd say, "We're still going to have a 'daddy adventure,' but first, I want to sit here on this bench for a moment." Then I'd asked them, "When we got out of the car and walked towards the mall, what did you notice? What did you see? What did you hear? What did you feel?"

The first time I did this, they looked at me dumbfounded, as I would have expected. They were born with curious, positive personalities, but their character, their self-awareness, and their situational awareness had not yet been developed. As a consequence, they really didn't have much to say.

Then I would tell them what I noticed: a mother and a father arguing, a dog barking, and a lady struggling to get her bags loaded into her car, and perhaps another vehicle had screeched its wheels and nearly run into another car. Once I told them all of this, the girls would say to me, "Dad, we didn't notice any of that."

Rather excitedly, I would say, "Here's what we're gonna do…" and then I would make a game out of it, just like Stran did at 12 years old with his alarm clock. "We're going back to the car, and then we'll drive to the other side of the mall. Now, don't get me wrong. We're gonna have an incredible day together. You're gonna get a new dress, you're gonna get a new pair of shoes, and you are gonna get that goldfish that I know you've wanted for so long."

When we got to the other side of the mall, I would park far away again. Then I would hold the hands of the two younger girls, and the older girl, this time, would walk a little more slowly than she had previously, and we would go to the other bench in front of the mall entrance. Once the four of us were sitting there, I would ask them, "What did you observe, girls?"

Dr. Carol Dweck wrote a great book called *Mindset*. I often use this book when I work with corporations, teams, athletic departments, or businesses. As Dr. Dweck would say, I was training their *seeing skills*, their situational awareness. It was stunning to me to watch how, at very early ages—four, five, seven, and nine—the girls would accurately tell me what they had noticed.

I didn't want our girls to have their eyes on their phones with their heads down and not realize they were actually on the X (in danger).

Then, we would go into the mall and have a great day doing all the things that we said we would do. However, now our daughters were armed with situational awareness and self-awareness and were prepared to act on the information that they had learned. Little did I know that 15 years later, our youngest daughter, while attending a very respectable, safe university in the great state of Texas, would use this training to save her own life.

She was 21 years old and in her junior year. While driving a white Ford Taurus with one of her sorority sisters in the passenger seat, she was stopped at a red light on campus. A motorcycle pulled up next to her, and the driver was wearing a red headband across his forehead, a leather jacket, a long-sleeved flannel shirt, jeans, and black boots with a chain. He reached into his pocket, pulled out a pistol, and pointed it at my daughter.

Her friend said, "Is that a gun?" In an instant, my daughter realized that she had a decision to make. She was on the X. Her amygdala fired up, and she knew she either had to fight or flee. Her sorority sister was in shock and froze, but my daughter quickly saw an exit avenue (always leave yourself an exit) and made a hard left, but not after getting a good look at the man on the motorcycle. I had taught her to look at the shoes, as they are the most difficult thing to change, so she did, and then she got off the X. She decided flight was the best decision, not fight—although later she would tell me that she considered turning the car into the motorcycle.

She went straight to the police station, gave a full description of what occurred, and then called me. I was in the car with former Major League Baseball player Jeff Frye (who had a remarkable career. I plan to write another book with Jeff, aka "Frito." Like Stran's story, Jeff's is equally compelling). We were headed to a fundraiser, and Jeff was driving. My phone rang, and it was our youngest daughter. Because we had practiced this, because we had trained, she knew to lead with, "Dad, I'm okay." Then, she explained exactly what had occurred.

At that point, the emotions came, and she began to cry a bit, but not until she had given a full description to the police and called me to let me know she was okay. The police officer then took the phone and told me exactly what was going to happen. After hanging up, I made a phone call to a friend who was in that area, and the pistol puller had a bad afternoon.

Have situational awareness and self-awareness, and then act. Having the courage (heart) to act, especially when new information is presented, is hard to do. *It must be trained, but it could save your life or that of your child. Train them well.*

FISHING WITH DENNY

Who would have thought that fishing would be a leadership laboratory for me? I had the privilege of fishing with a gentleman named Denny Brauer, who's in the Professional Bass Fishing Hall of Fame. He's a remarkable man. He lives on Lake Amistad in Del Rio, Texas. I've had the privilege of meeting many well-known artists, performers, and professional athletes, but only three have gotten me choked up. One was a U.S. president, the other was actor Gary Sinise at West Point, and the third was Denny Brauer, the only professional bass fisherman to have ever appeared on the Wheaties box (trivia win right there).

I had the privilege of fishing with Denny one day on Lake Amistad. In fact, we have fished several times since then, and he's become a dear friend. However, that first day, Denny said something that I'll always remember, and Stran actually said the same thing to me at a later date. We fished all morning on Lake Amistad. I didn't say much at all, and neither did Denny. Denny was at the front of the boat, and I was in the back, and I was as nervous as a long-tailed cat around a fireplace. I was fishing with a guy I had seen on TV, a childhood icon for me.

For four hours that morning, Denny caught a lot of fish. I forget how many, but I caught two. Finally, he said, "We're going to eat lunch." He pulled his brand-new bass boat onto a sandy embankment. After pulling out two bologna sandwiches, two bags of yellow potato chips, and two cans of Dr. Pepper, he looked at me and said, "You're a good fisherman, and you've got a lot to learn. This morning, I noticed that you *missed* a lot of fish. I could hear what was going on in the back of the boat." He had extraordinary situational awareness. "Why do you think that is?"

I responded like most would, saying something along the lines of, "I'm throwing the wrong lure," "I'm throwing the wrong color," and "I'm fishing too fast or too slow."

Then he said this: "The fish are *interested* in what you're doing, but they're not *committed*. There's a difference between being interested and committed. You've got to determine how to get those fish to be fully committed to what you're doing. The only reason I have out-fished you is that I've been able to get the fish to commit, and you have not. You may be committed to fishing (working hard), but you've got to adjust to get the fish equally committed to your lure."

I was speechless. Of course, he was right, and I needed to adjust to the fish, the audience, and the other members of this event. Named leaders in official positions of power need to adjust to the people they are trying to reach, inspire, serve, and lead.

After we finished our lunch, I watched how he fished, observing everything that he was doing. Without knowing it, he was presenting me with a leadership laboratory on how to get fish, of all things, to commit. After watching him, my afternoon was a lot more successful than my morning.

The next day, we fished again, and I was still at the back of the boat. At first, I caught more fish than the great Denny Brauer. I had figured out how to get the fish to commit—I let them. But just as I started thinking, *I'm gonna beat Denny Brauer,* he became the Hall of Famer that he was before my eyes. The truth is, I had no shot. Ego had crept into my mind. I *had* gotten the fish to commit, but I hadn't managed my ego. Ryan Holiday wrote a great book called *Ego is the Enemy.* I recommend it. In his book, Ryan writes about how even the slightest bit of ego can be a threat to derail an otherwise incredible opportunity or path to success. He's one of the best writers I've ever read.

At the end of the day, Denny had beaten me by six or seven fish. We had a laugh that evening at dinner. Denny and I have become great friends. One of the great compliments of my life as a fisherman was when Denny stopped everybody at dinner and said, "Hey, the Colonel can fish. Don't ever doubt that."

"Our thoughts are our way of communicating with ourselves. Serve yourself wisely with your thoughts—thoughts are 100% choice. Thoughts trigger action. Before an action occurs, there is a thought, even if it is a split-second thought."
–J. Craig Flowers

COMMUNICATION:

I've never been asked by an organization to come in because their communication is so great. No one has ever called me and said, "Hello, Craig. We're struggling with communication. We communicate way too well. Could you help us at our upcoming executive retreat on how not to communicate so well?"

The elite communicate so effectively that it's rarely an issue. They practice communicating. Literally, they practice it. Pilots even practice their tone when making radio communications. How many businesses do you know that *practice* communicating? That really commit, once a month, to professional development training, which includes how we communicate—email, text, face-to-face, phone, etc.? Most don't do it. The elite DO.

I was reminded of this in 1988 when I was part of a military operation called Nimrod Dancer. The name is a bit odd—I didn't pick it. This was the prelude, the "show of force" mission for what would later become Operation Just Cause. Coincidentally, the Green Beret that I work out with every morning led an A-team for Operation Just Cause. Each day, I was flown across the Panama Canal to update our battalion, which was going through jungle warfare school, on what was happening on the other side of the canal.

It was just a two-man helicopter (OH-58), and each day, I became closer friends with the pilot, a warrant officer. As we flew back and forth across the Panama Canal, sometimes, we'd listen to a Major League Baseball game, of all things. It was surreal. But I got to know the pilot very well, and one day, he asked me, "Would you like to fly the aircraft?"

I thought, *Of course*. I was perhaps 25 years old. I said, "Sure, I would love to."

"Now, listen," he said. "There's one thing that we are going to do that is not open for discussion. When I give you the controls, I'm going to say, 'You have the controls,' and I need you to say back to me, 'I have the controls.' Then you will hear me say, 'You have the controls.' Three-way communication." Then we practiced it—we repped it—so there was no doubt who had the controls. He emphasized this was not open for discussion. It had to be done exactly like this.

A few seconds later, he said, "Are you ready?" I told him I was, and he said, "You have the controls."

"I have the controls," I replied.

"You have the controls," he repeated. Then, for a couple of minutes, I held the controls of this two-person helicopter, and we flew across the Panama Canal. When I gave him the controls back, we went through that same communication process.

Communication is one of the hallmarks of the elite. They use a technique called the "back brief." After the leader has communicated his intent, everyone looks for their specific tasks and implied tasks, something that I will get to a little later. Then the leader listens to the back brief to make sure that what he or she has communicated is clearly understood. They do this routinely. For the average, the good, and even the great, their blind spot is often communication. I tried this with my wife when "we" kept losing car keys. "You have the keys…" It didn't go as smoothly as the helicopter ride in Panama, but "we" stopped losing the keys!

I'm reminded of this great story I heard about the legendary Alabama football coach Bear Bryant telling his offensive coordinator, "Run the reverse. Run the reverse. Run the darn reverse!" He repeated it four or five times. Finally, the offensive coordinator called for and ran the reverse. When the running back was tackled immediately in the backfield for a loss, Bear Bryant said, "Not to that side!!!" The elite start with themselves.

If there's any failure or setback in the mission, they'll often find that if they search in concentric circles, they'll discover a solution that is a lot closer to them than they may have previously even considered. A three-star general taught me this, General Lawson W. Magruder III, who said, "When things go wrong, no matter who's at fault, no matter who's responsible, start with yourself."

How many of us reading this book have had something like this happen in the last 24 hours: You can't find your hotel room key, wallet, purse, or sunglasses, only to realize that the sunglasses are on your head, the wallet is in your other pair of pants, or the purse is hanging behind the pantry door, which is closed. The elite start with themselves, and they'll often find a solution to their problem that's a lot closer to them than they may have even considered. And often, it's communication.

SPECIFIC TASKS AND IMPLIED TASKS: WHAT'S THE DIFFERENCE?

Previously, we talked about not hitting the snooze button and getting the first victory of the day. That is a very specific task. The moment they wake up, the elite go 1-0 each and every day by not hitting that snooze button. It's a simple act, and they don't think about it; they simply execute. Then, they immediately start hunting for associated implied tasks.

Remember when Stran was 12 years old? Well, not only did he ask for an alarm clock, but he had plenty of chores to do that day, just like all of us when we were 12 years old. When I was young, like most children, I was often asked to take the trash out. When my mom asked, "Craig, did you take the trash out?" I would say, "Yes, Mom. I did. I took the trash out. Jeez."

Then she would quietly say, "Did you put a sack back in the trash can?"

"Well, you didn't ask me to do that."

"No, son. That was *implied*."

What we know about the elite is that they execute *specific* tasks with extraordinary precision, timeliness, and accuracy. Then, without being asked, they immediately start hunting for the associated *implied* task. With every specific task, there is most assuredly an *implied* task. This is part of their routine, a part of their process. And when everyone on a team executes specific tasks and starts hunting for and executing implied tasks, oh, that's when the magic happens. Suddenly, things start getting done that were never accomplished before. That certainly won't happen with average organizations or average people, which, by definition, make up the majority.

CONSTRUCTIVE VS. INSTRUCTIVE

Danny Akers was the fourth-string quarterback for the University of Texas. His father was the head coach, Fred Akers. Danny never expected to play, but in one particular game against Baylor University, after the first-, second-, and third-string quarterbacks became injured, duty called. Akers didn't have a mouthpiece and couldn't find his helmet.

The first snap was a fumble under center. The second snap was also a fumble under center. And the third snap was also a fumble under center. You can imagine the crowd at the University of Texas. But as Danny lay there, hovering over the football after that third fumble, he noticed the ref throw a yellow flag. He had been hit late by a linebacker for Baylor. It was a 15-yard penalty and automatic first down. He looked back at the sidelines, and the third-string quarterback had caught his breath and was coming back out on the field. As Danny ran off the field with the "Hook 'em Horns" hand sign held high, the stadium announcer said, "FIRST DOWN, Texas," and the crowd went crazy.

Danny passed away a few years ago, but not before we had a great discussion. He was a good friend, and we talked about the difference between *instructive* and *constructive* organizations. He was determined to become an elite member of society, and he, too, had studied leadership after his playing days at the University of Texas. He was curious to know how the elite operated. I shared this idea with him.

Most of the average, good, and even great organizations are instructive. What I mean by that is that someone is in a position of power or authority, a colonel, general, CEO, or president. They tell you what to do, and you do it or else. In these organizations, there's a lot of fear, doom, anxiety, and caution. Among the elite, however, there's a lot of trust, confidence, and will to get things done.

The root word for "constructive" is "construct." To put it in sports terms, an instructive coach might say, "If you don't make that block, this play will never work." A constructive coach, however, would say, "When you make that block, this play will succeed."

Sometimes, elite organizations are instructive, mostly when safety is involved. But for the most part, and I believe it to be around 80%, they are constructive. They construct one another, and with that, the second and third-order effects become trust, confidence, and faith, and a culture emerges, a constructive culture, an elite culture, one in which members of the organization execute specific tasks with precision and accuracy and immediately start hunting the implied task. Why? Because they know that every member of the team is doing the exact same thing. They are behaving constructively.

There are times, such as when raising a child, when we must be instructive: "Do not cross that street, or else." With any company that has a high risk of injury, for example, there are times when it must be instructive (again, safety). For the most part, however, we want innovative, creative, and courageous folks who are constructive. In constructive organizations, there are a lot of elite behaviors and very little tolerance for ego.

I truly believe that these leadership laboratories are all around us. The Colonel has talked a lot already about being 1–0 to start your day. Matthew 6:33 says, *"Seek ye first the kingdom of God and all these things will be added unto you."* Well, if we take that advice literally, we need to seek God first. God is the ultimate positive. Seek the good first. Lead with that, and always seek the harder right over the easier wrong. The Colonel will hit on that later in the book.

Here's an example of how, when I was in my early teens, I took a task and made it my own. We lived 20 miles from a small rural town in Texas called Tell, out in the middle of nowhere, and we had an extremely large concrete back porch. One of my tasks was to sweep the sand off that porch. Now, like most kids, I didn't like to sweep, but I took something that I really didn't like to do and mixed in something that I love to do. I love to compete. I love to compete against anybody. I wanted to keep score. That was my M.O.—let's play a game and keep score. Now, if you beat me, that's good. I wasn't a sore loser. I just wanted to compete. I made a game of sweeping the back porch. I timed myself.

I graded myself. And over months, even years, of doing this, I turned into not just a good sweeper, but a really *great* sweeper. I even told myself as I did it, sweating in the 115-degree heat in Tell, Texas, that I was the best sweeper in the world. I spoke those words aloud.

They say that the strongest words you will ever hear are the ones that come out of your own mouth. As I swept that back porch, which would probably be covered in sand 15 minutes later because the wind always blows in Tell, I was training myself to be the very best at something that really didn't matter in the broad scheme of life. But now, looking back, I think it set a foundation for me that I relied on later in life. I not only took something that I didn't like to do and wasn't very good at doing, but I made myself one of the best there was at it because I told myself I was, I graded myself, and I timed myself. How much easier it was to work harder at things when I was in my 20s and 30s, especially when they were things that I loved to do.

Stran talks about leadership laboratories being all around us. They certainly are. Think about your own home. None of us like to empty the dishwasher. In fact, many of us, when the dishwasher is filled with clean dishes, and I've done this myself, we'll open up the dishwasher, grab our favorite coffee mug, and then shut the dishwasher quickly and leave the house. You see teenagers do this often, not just with a dishwasher, but a dryer full of clean clothes. They open the dryer, grab their favorite t-shirt, shut the dryer quickly, and run out of the house. The elite, on the other hand, look at these things as leadership laboratories, something that we'll talk about in the next chapter, an opportunity to develop character and the prefrontal cortex when the average aren't even aware of it.

None of us like to sweep the porch. Stran certainly did not. None of us like to empty the dishwasher. But if we have the situational awareness and the self-awareness to view these things as leadership laboratories, as opportunities to practice discipline and develop behaviors and routines, suddenly, that dishwasher will get empty. The most difficult part is the knives and forks. And if a teenager sees one of their friends emptying a dishwasher, of course, they're going to chip in and start helping.

That's what a true friend would do. That's what you would do.

No one likes to fold cleaned clothes, but if you look at a dryer full of clothes as an opportunity to practice character and discipline as a leadership laboratory, suddenly, they get folded rather quickly. Whether it's taking out the trash or writing a thank-you note, leadership laboratories are all around us. The elite recognize them not as chores or things that they must do but as things that they should do because the average, the majority, do not. They love to rep discipline and character.

Choosing the harder right over the easier wrong. I never thought that those words from the West Point Cadet Prayer would be repeated by a cowboy in Childress, Texas.

Scan the QR code for bonus video content!

Bonus Video Content!

CHAPTER 4

Character Reps vs. Physical Reps

"I had no choice but to rep character. All of my physical reps were simply not enough, and most of the time, I was injured. Through my thoughts, prayers, behavior, and actions, I was practicing/repping character without realizing it."
–Stran T Smith

• • •

BLUF: Practicing Character builds enduring Character.
Like building muscle. It's that simple. Look for and
execute #CharacterReps.

• • •

THE IMPORTANCE OF CHARACTER

The prefrontal cortex is critical to winning; it's why so many of us in our early 20s and even teenage years, specifically young men, make so many mistakes. See, the prefrontal cortex serves as a hard drive for the rest of our lives, and it needs to be trained just like every other part of your body.

Let's take a look at the NFL Combine. In the Combine, the NFL tests college football players mentally and physically. When it comes to strength, they record how many times a player can bench press two 45-pound plates on each side of a 45-pound bar, 225 pounds in all. But what about 225 pounds of character? How many times has that been lifted or practiced?

Leaders often mistakenly assume that just because someone is part of an organization or team, they will somehow develop into a person of character. When I work specifically with football coaches who want me to keep it simple, I ask them to talk about their culture. I ask them to talk about their team's character. So many times, they think that just yelling or being more colorful with language will develop character. It will not. Character must be practiced. It must be repped. Yelling "mother-frogger" at players does NOT build their character, but it sure reveals yours. And it's lazy.

The beautiful thing about a character rep is that, unlike a physical rep, it's always the right thing to do, and it has the added advantage of developing one's character. For example, if we ran a marathon today, we're not going to run a marathon tomorrow. We have to rest and recover. When Stran had a stroke or blew out his shoulder, the next day, he was not going to rope. Physical reps are necessary to compete in the rodeo arena, but they're not always the right thing to do.

But a character rep is always the right thing to do. I tell coaches, "If you want 225 pounds of character to show up, your athletes have to start lifting the bar of character." Character is developed, so build in character reps. One thing I appreciated about the military, particularly during the ten years I spent supporting the most elite military personnel on the planet, is that they always scheduled professional development experiences. They were called Officer Professional Development (OPDs). I grew to enjoy them. Each OPD was organized and executed by a different officer (sometimes a junior officer). We were all there to get better, and we did. They lasted about an hour, and afterward, we had a few beverages. This is key—they were scheduled 12 months out. Meaning in January, the OPD schedule was published.

They commit to them once a month. Yes, some tactical training, and perhaps some reading, was part of those professional development experiences. However, for the most part, it was all about behavior and character. These soldiers were practicing the behavior that they needed to show up during the most critical times of a mission.

My grandfather used to say, "Let's have an understanding before we have a misunderstanding." I never knew quite what that meant until I got older. Let's practice those behaviors together, all while developing our prefrontal cortex and becoming not only tactically and physically developed but also behaviorally, i.e., with character reps.

At the time of writing, I am working with two presidents of a publicly traded company, one that you would recognize. In fact, I exchanged emails with them this morning. While I have instructed them on their tactical daily routines, we will soon get into the development of the behaviors required to lead (serve) a team to elite levels of success. They don't know it yet, but at the end of this six- or seven-month experience, also known as executive coaching, they will be fundamentally changed when it comes to how they view behaviors.

They will learn to view behaviors as a competitive edge. I've had the privilege of working with several Fortune 500 companies, one of which is a computer business that a gentleman started in his garage in Austin, TX. I explained to his senior staff, "The profits that you are looking for are not in the margins. They are in the behaviors and processes of the people you bring on board. What is your plan to develop an agreed-upon set of behaviors and practice those behaviors so that they show up, not just in and around the main building in Austin, Texas, but all over the world where your products are sold?"

The beautiful thing about repping character is that there are opportunities all around us to practice. One could say that not hitting the snooze button is a character rep, making you 1–0 first thing in the morning. Character reps also include simple things around our home and office, such as emptying a dishwasher when we don't feel like it because it's not something we normally do or writing a thank-you note to that person who has been on our mind. Remember, the beautiful thing about a character rep is that it's the right thing to do and develops one's character.

The West Point Cadet Prayer is powerful. One of the lines says, "Make us choose the harder right instead of the *easier wrong*." So many times, a character rep is simply choosing the *harder right*. What's funny about choosing the harder right is that, often, it's not hard at all. It just takes a little situational awareness and self-awareness and then having the courage, the heart, to take action.

I had the privilege of working with the Air It Out Football Academy in Abilene, Texas, where we train young men in high school and junior high—and we've had a couple of females as well at the quarterback and receiver positions (where Stran and I first met). After the first session, sometime around 2014, when I was first asked to speak, the founder of Air It Out, Coach Alan Wartes, asked me what my observations were. I told him, "Well, you've got plenty of physical reps, but you have very few character reps built into your program." He asked me to go on., and I said, "Part of your experience needs to be a handwritten thank-you note."

"What do you mean by that?" he asked.

Each summer, Air It Out hosts thousands of football players from around the great state of Texas, and some come from as far away as New York. "Every one of these players is going to develop physically because of the Air It Out program," I explained, "but what are you doing to develop their prefrontal cortexes, their *seeing* skills? A handwritten thank you note, something that takes less than a couple of minutes to write, will contribute to that development. It will also be a great marketing tool, by the way, because, in so many cases, this will be the only thank-you note that a 15-year-old has written in the last 12 months."

These thank-you notes are actually historical documents. As you're reading this right now, I am certain that somewhere in your home or office, in a drawer, you have one, two, or a handful of thank-you notes that someone has written you. At home, a thank-you note has probably been magnetized to the refrigerator to be seen nearly every day. It seems like a small thing, but a thank-you note is more than just a note of thanks. It's the right thing to do, yes, but it's also a character rep—and repping character is the harder right over the easier wrong. It's a blind spot for the average person, which creates a great opportunity for everybody else.

TRAINING BEHAVIORS

When I have the opportunity to work with businesses and corporations, I always try to incorporate a training scenario where we practice behavior, specifically communication. I break down facial expressions, body language—all of that. Participants have to speak in front of their peers. This is a training developmental experience. I tell them, "Despite your boss being in the room, this is not punitive in any way. This is developmental." Now, this requires bosses to be understanding, but hey, they're the ones who asked for a developmental experience in the first place. Elite teams are always developing. Training scenarios in business should not be driven by numbers or Excel spreadsheets but by scenarios that require a reaction to success, failure, and new information.

The elite do this really well. They *schedule* this training, rely on it, and anchor themselves to it. They know that they will get better when this training is scheduled. In average organizations, when training is on the organizational calendar, most people typically roll their eyes and go in with their iPhones charged or their laptops open and pretend like they're paying attention, but not the elite. The elite are present and eager to get better.

Whenever I give a keynote address, provide leader development training, or participate in a retreat for an organization, I lead with, "If you come out of here with one, two, or three things to go back and implement into your life or your organization, it's a win, a competitive edge." Then I'll say, "By the way, each and every one of you is communicating with me, nonverbally, right now."

Many times when average organizations schedule leadership training, many arrive with a mindset of "Let's just get through this so we can have a nice dinner, get some swag, and get back to the things that we have been doing over the last quarter or fiscal year." The right behaviors, however, provide a competitive edge. Training scenarios that develop the behaviors required to become elite, such as communication and repping character, are critical, yet they're often overlooked. One of the first things that gets cut during a difficult economy is professional development training. However, this is not the case for the elite. The elite invest in *more* leader development because they KNOW it's an advantage during uncertain times.

The elite double down on training, especially during difficult times. They know that as staff members are cut, training becomes a critical element to the organization's success. The elite demand such training, and they wonder why it's not scheduled. If they see that the leader is not willing to schedule it, they take the initiative to schedule it themselves and invite the leader.

That's why only 4% are among the elite.

Scan the QR code for bonus video content!

Bonus Video Content!

CHAPTER 5

Know, Care, Then Challenge

"Men who sit back and pride themselves on their culture haven't any to speak of."
–Ralph Waldo Emerson, *"Civilization," Society and Solitude,* 1870

• • •

BLUF: Members of elite teams know one another like no others and care for one another like no others; therefore, they can challenge one another like no others.

• • •

THE FORMULA FOR THE ELITE

In 1991, I was an Army captain and company commander. We lived in Maryland. The phone rang one day, and my wife answered. I could tell right away it was somebody important. One of the most influential people in my life was calling—Lieutenant General Lawson W. Magruder III, my former brigade commander in the 25th Infantry Division. I had not spoken to him for six or seven years.

After some greetings, Miss Beth covered the mouthpiece, looked at me, and said, "It's General Magruder." I literally stood at attention in our kitchen.

I took the phone, and in a calm, confident, deep voice, General Magruder said, "Hello, Craig. Are you taking *care* of your soldiers?"

Know, Care, and *Challenge* IS THE FORMULA for the elite—in that order. Most people and organizations have this formula in the exact opposite order: I'm in a position of authority. I tell you what to do (challenge), and you do it or else. I'm going to act like I care about you by asking how your day is in the break room while you're warming up before practice or after you've come home from school. I'm going to act like I *know* you and your spouse at the annual Christmas party. *Know, Care,* and *then Challenge* is a formula that is simply not negotiable for the 4%, also known as the elite. This simple formula can be applied to families, communities, teams, and even individuals. Let's look at Stran Smith.

With the loss of his friend, members of his team, and not one but two horses, Stran immediately defaulted to what the average do: he challenged himself to drive countless hours to work harder, which, as we know, is not a process. He claims to have stayed awake for seven days straight without sleep, repeatedly challenging himself, neglecting his well-being, and lacking any self-awareness—and why would he? He had an underdeveloped prefrontal cortex that was driven simply by discipline, hard work, and, frankly, a series of significant emotional events.

He was drained completely. The truth is, although he had elite talent, he had little chance of winning the World Championship and achieving elite success. He was not caring for his body. He was simply challenging himself, and the result was that he ended up passing out on the floor with one sock on. No know or care, only challenge.

General Magruder retired from the Army as a three-star general. He, too, has written a book, which he sent me just a few months ago, and I stayed up all night reading it. In the book, he emphasizes this same simple formula. Working with NCAA coaches and staff, I've shared the *Know, Care,* then *Challenge* formula. We teach this during sessions lasting two to three days. (Note: Stran and I will soon host leadership conferences in Childress, Texas, and across the country).

Some put the *Know, Care, Challenge* formula in play; it becomes a competitive edge, and they win. Others—because of ego, I've found—discard the formula, calling it soft. They are willfully stubborn and ignorant for stating such nonsense. For those who take it seriously, they not only win but enjoy their work even more. Many, however, do what Stran did. They spend more time in the office, looking at film and studying schemes and plays. They simply rope more calves and go without sleep, believing that's the answer.

I've never met Chris Petersen, but I believe he is one of the greatest leaders of men I have ever seen in college football. He coached at Boise State and Washington University. He only recruited talented players who were "OKGs" (Our Kind of Guys). He won over and over again. He knew them, he cared for them, and when he challenged them, they responded.

ADAPTING TO CHANGE

The formula's effectiveness is even true when it comes to our families, and I was reminded of this recently in New Braunfels, Texas, where I was speaking. I offered an evening session with parents of student-athletes, and that evening, the parent session was packed. One particular parent showed up with their son, a senior in high school who was the captain of the football team. The young man was seated right next to his mom, and I was so glad that they had both come to the event that I decided to take a risk while on stage.

When I introduced the *Know, Care,* then *Challenge* formula to the audience, I paused for a moment and looked at this mom and son. I said, "Mom, without looking at your son, tell me what his favorite color is."

She smiled broadly, her eyes lit up, and she said, "Oh, his favorite color is red."

As soon as she completed that sentence, her son's head snapped to the right. He looked at her and said, "Mom, my favorite color is blue!"

The *Know, Care, Challenge* formula requires understanding that people evolve. That young man's favorite color at some point in his life, likely when he was five, six, seven, perhaps even 10 years old, was, in fact, red. But as the

Christmas trees passed year after year, the young man's favorite color changed.

So many times, whether you're a leader in business, a parent, or coaching a sports team, you have to accept that knowing somebody at a certain point in their life is not knowing them where they are today. Today, that young man's favorite color is blue.

My own mother had me at the age of 19 and now resides in Weatherford, Texas. When I was a young boy, I loved—and when I say love, I mean I *loved*—chocolate-covered raisins. But over the years, my taste changed. I no longer like chocolate-covered raisins, yet every Christmas, I get a wonderful package from my mother with chocolate-covered raisins. It's not because she doesn't love me; it's simply because she thinks I still like chocolate-covered raisins. I've never told her that I don't any longer. Hopefully, she'll learn about it by reading this book. Maybe it'll even save her a few dollars each Christmas.

Know, Care, and then *Challenge.* Leaders must use that formula. We all change. We all develop. We have different tastes. We have different desires. We have different goals. If I had told Stran Smith at the age of 25, "This is the formula to winning the World Championship," he would have been resistant. A hijacked amygdala drove him. He was driven only by emotion and what he knew, which was that he had to work harder than anyone else in the world, just like many high school and NCAA coaches. And that's a given fact; he did have to work harder than anybody else in the world. But at the same time, he had to know his body. He had to care how his body functioned. Only then could he *challenge* himself.

THE IMPORTANCE OF RECOVERY

To play athletics, to do anything physical, one has to practice. These are called physical reps. We have to know that if we ran a marathon yesterday, our bodies would not be prepared to run a marathon today. If we lifted heavy weights yesterday, we're not prepared to lift extremely heavy weights today. Our bodies have to rest and recover.

Our minds have to heal and absorb what we just experienced. That's part of the know and care part of the process. Stran had the challenge piece down, no doubt. He was going to work as hard as he possibly could all the way to the point of passing out. What I know from my experiences in the army is that after about two and a half days, you start to hallucinate. I've done this in the jungles of Panama and other places. The body simply shuts down, and that's what happened with Stran. He was not at his full capacity.

Why? Because he simply didn't *know*, and he hadn't *cared* for his body. It's not always the right time to rep something physically. We may be nursing an injury—like Stran and his shoulder, for example. We may have a broken collarbone, a broken leg, or an illness. The best thing we can do then is care for that illness (Change of Mission). If we broke our collarbone yesterday, we're not going to lift weights tomorrow. *Know, Care, Challenge* is a formula the elite use.

ONBOARDING A NEW TEAM MEMBER:

I worked recently with a publicly traded bank; it was their annual retreat. We were talking about hiring and onboarding new personnel, something they really wanted to get right. Most organizations have a 90-day onboarding process. What's important during those 90 days is the new employee, the newest member of the team, administratively gets on board. They receive training on software, perhaps, or on vocabulary that the company uses. At the end of that 90 days, it is assumed that they are ready to go to work. They are not. The 91st day is now the most important day.

Throughout those 90 days, it's interesting to watch how veterans of the team behave. They see the new employee walking nervously through the hallways, and they greet them, but then privately, when they head to their other offices, they say, "Did you see the new person? They looked completely lost." Sometimes, they even chuckle and add, "Yeah, that's how I felt, too, in my first two weeks." Then, under their breath, perhaps in the break room, they say, "Oh, they'll figure it out." That's average behavior. Let's look at how an elite team may do it differently.

BLAKE AND PEYTON

I was reminded of this with the great story of Peyton Manning, arguably one of the best quarterbacks to have ever played the game of football, a Hall of Famer. Later in his career, he was traded to the Denver Broncos. What's interesting about the NFL roster is that there's another roster associated with those 53 players, the practice squad. Depending on the organization, the practice squad numbers anywhere from eight to 12 players. Peyton Manning arrived in Denver and was comfortably settled in with his new team members. They were excited to have this elite leader and quarterback. Their goal was to win a Super Bowl.

But there was another player, signed to the Broncos' practice squad—Blake Gideon. I've told this story for years, but before we wrote this book, I wanted to make sure I had it exactly right, so I called Blake Gideon's father in Central Texas, and he shared this story with me.

Blake was a very successful college athlete who played for the University of Texas. He arrived at the Denver Broncos practice facility, where he was onboarded quickly, given his gear, shown where his locker was, etc. Keep in mind, he was only a member of the *practice* squad, not the 53-person Denver roster. At around 11 a.m., the administrator said, "The team is out practicing right now. Go ahead and go to the cafeteria. When the team finishes their morning practice, they'll join you for lunch."

Our last active-duty assignment was at West Point. Before they take a new instructor and put them in front of cadets, we're trained in the art and science of pedagogy—how to teach. They also talk about the behavior of cadets, down to the latest detail. We are told the cadet who does not want to get called upon or singled out will almost always sit in the far back right of the room. Well, Blake Gideon went through the cafeteria line, filled his tray with great nutrition, and then moved to the far back right of the cafeteria—you know, where the new kid or employee sits (just watch the next time you are in a room for a conference or during a meeting).

Pretty soon, the rest of the Denver Broncos finished practice and began to filter into the cafeteria. I imagine the defensive backs were the first to go through the line, chatting as they got their food and then found a place to sit together. In my mind, I have them seated in the far left of the cafeteria. They knew one another already, leaving the newest member of the organization seated alone. Another position group arrived, and they all sat together in the center of the room, laughing, joking, and prodding one another as athletes often do. You get the idea. Then, finally, Peyton Manning arrived. But then, after filling his tray with food, he paused.

He wanted to be *situationally aware* and *self-aware* and then take *action*. Peyton Manning saw the newest member of the Denver Broncos practice squad, somebody he did not know, Blake Gideon, seated alone. He glanced over at the other two position groups, enjoying their lunch and the brotherhood of athletics, and then went directly to the newest member of the organization, the newest hire, the new student, the new kid, and sat down and introduced himself by first and last name.

Think of the second- and third-order effects. When the rest of the Denver Broncos' 53-person roster arrived for lunch, I imagine they asked themselves, "Who's Peyton sitting with over there?" Soon, the newest member of the *practice squad* was joined by other members of the 53-person roster, including the offensive line and receivers, and now the newest employee, the newest practice squad member, was being introduced in a way he'd never been before. Peyton Manning told Blake, "We're so glad that you're here. You're gonna help us win a Super Bowl. You play an extraordinarily important role for us." Can you imagine how that new employee, Blake Gideon, must have felt? He called his parents that night to tell them what had happened.

Of course, as the great Paul Harvey once said, "And now you know the rest of the story." The Denver Broncos did win the Super Bowl that year. Blake

Gideon played an important role as a member of the practice squad, inspired by a lunch meeting on his first day at work with the most talented, most respected member of the team, Peyton Manning, who, on that road to a Super Bowl championship, was named the most valuable player.

One can go back and watch the interview of Peyton Manning as he stands on that platform with confetti falling down, and as he's asked what it feels like to be the MVP and win the Super Bowl, he immediately thinks of every member of the Denver Broncos organization, the coaches, the practice squad members, the entire team, the administrators, the trainers. Peyton wanted to make sure that he knew and that he cared. Then he could challenge every member of the organization. They won. How do you treat the new kid, employee, player, teacher, or coach?

EXEMPLIFYING THE FORMULA

Stran Smith had not been introduced to the *Know, Care, Challenge* philosophy, but he watched it play out over and over through his wife, Jennifer. Jennifer is one of those special people who is situationally aware when she walks into a room. She notices every person there and looks for anyone who is trying to be invisible.

One example of this is the story of how Jen met one of her best friends, Kellie. It was 2003, and Kellie was an unpaid intern assigned to make copies of results in the media room at a big rodeo in Omaha, Nebraska. Jen was the sideline reporter for ESPN, someone who, to a young rodeo queen and journalist like Kellie, was a glamorous celebrity. Imagine Kellie's surprise when Jennifer made her way to the copy machine and, within a matter of minutes, knew Kellie's life story.

A few months later, the same scenario played out in Dallas. This time, though, Jen greeted Kellie with a hug, remembered her name, and asked about the things Kellie had told her in Omaha. Jennifer has the extraordinary ability to make everyone around her feel like the most important person in the room, and through her actions, she demonstrated that she knew and cared, and that was inspiring. When Kellie wanted to practice her photography skills several years later, she felt comfortable enough to reach out to Jen, and the rest, as they say, is history. Kellie has become not only the Smith's family photographer, but also a close friend. She and Jennifer have reached the "challenge" phase of their relationship, where they challenge and encourage one another, and they are both better for it. Iron sharpens iron.

Stran watched scenarios play out like this over and over through Jennifer, but it wasn't until he met Dodd Romero that he got to experience the *Know, Care, and Challenge* formula for himself. "He spent time with me, knowing me, knowing my sport, knowing my event, knowing my needs physically, spiritually, and emotionally, then he started to care and love me," Stran said. "And then he was my brother. Once we reached that stage in our relationship, it was easy to allow Dodd to have the authority to speak into my life."

For me, knowing, caring, and challenging speaks to the importance of relationships. I realized when I met Dodd that if I was ever going to be able to accomplish anything of any significance, it was going to have not as much to do with me as it was going to have to do with the people that I surrounded myself with.

You have to "know" someone before you can "care" for that person and before you can "challenge" them. No matter what you're dealing with, whether it's yourself, a team, a coworker, or, in my case, a horse, you have to know them before you can care for them, and then you can challenge them. I'm careful about who I give authority to speak into my life. This principle is so important to us that we have made it one of our unspoken bylaws of STS, and that is "Never let a problem be bigger than the relationship."

Our commitment to knowing and caring about people before we challenge them isn't just an STS principle; it's a biblical one. James 1:19 says,

"Be quick to listen, slow to speak, slow to anger." Well, if you reverse all that and are slow to listen and quick to anger, that throws everything into a tailspin, and all kinds of problems ensue—kind of like what would happen if you dialed 119 in an emergency instead of 911. It wouldn't work so well.

Your relationship with yourself is even more important than your relationship with others. If you start to challenge yourself before you really care for yourself and before you actually get to know who you are, that's when things go sideways.

When I met the Colonel for the first time, I was in a parent conference at the Air It Out Football Academy, and I knew that this was going to be a place that was perfect for both us and our kids. It was easy to see that Air It Out was built around relationships and family. I believe the truest form of relationship is family. I could see instantly that our values were going to align.

I could relate to their philosophy because that is exactly what I try to do with my roping clinics. We want to get to know people, then care for them, love on them, and then… guess what? Then we can challenge them. Meeting the Colonel at the Air It Out Academy was another demonstration of the *Know, Care, Challenge* philosophy. We built a relationship, and now I consider the Colonel and his family my family. And because we've built a relationship on knowing and caring about each other, we have become better people because we can challenge each other. That helps both of us become elite.

The Colonel now has the authority to speak into my life. Dodd has the authority to speak into my life. I think it's very important to carefully select the people you surround yourself with and whom you give authority to speak into your life. It is equally important to pay attention to who's NOT allowed to speak authority into your life.

There have been many times as a professional cowboy that I could've listened to the wrong authorities. At the NFR, there's an armchair quarterback in every autograph line, bathroom stall, and even behind the chutes. When you're doing well? They've got advice for how to continue the roll you're on.

When you start doing poorly? Boy, you better look out because suddenly, EVERYBODY is an expert. They'll tell you how to swing your rope, critique your dismount, and even suggest a different horse for you to ride. And if you're not careful, as crazy as it is, you start to question whether those armchair quarterbacks are right.

Thankfully, I surrounded myself with people who DID have the wisdom and authority to speak into me—my wife, my dad, Dodd. Those are the voices I had to discipline myself to listen to, and then I had to tune out the rest.

That's how important relationships are to me, and I try to protect and nurture the ones I have with the men and women I have given authority to speak into my life, what they do, and what they say to me.

In December of 2006, when I met Dodd in that hotel lobby, he told me, "In God's time, God will tell me when we need to start this mission. You go home and rest, relax, and recover. Let your body heal. I will call you when it's time."

For the next four months, I didn't hear from him. Finally, though, I got the phone call, and the next day, Jen and I jumped on a plane and flew to Miami. That was when this life-transformation journey started. Every minute with him was him loving us and learning about us, us learning about him, and him teaching me the correct way to cook and season my food.

We started in March 2007. Until December 2008, I'd bet I didn't have over 300 grams of sugar. We cut sugar completely out. Absolutely zero sugar. Zero whites (sugar OR carbs). Anything that was not healthy and good for you, we cut it out of the diet. Dodd taught Jen and me how to cook and eat clean. That was a term I didn't even know at the time. What is clean eating? Well, basically, all the taste comes out. It's really what that actually means.

However, with this transformation, good, clean food tasted so good to me. After a while, I didn't even desire oil, any kind of seasoning, or condiments. They were completely cut out. We ate nothing but grilled fish, grilled chicken, and grilled steak. I bet I ate a truckload of sweet potatoes, dry, with nothing on them but red pepper. I lived on boiled eggs—of course, without the yolk. Refried beans, brown rice, everything was very calculated, and I learned how to eat to live, not live to eat.

I also started seeing the importance of putting this nutrition in your body, devoting time to recovery, and working out in specific ways. The way I stretched, the way I did cardio, the way I prepared, and the way I rested were all important. Dodd told me that he was going to make me faster, stronger, slimmer, and more agile. When we started, I thought, *I just need to be able to learn how to swing my rope. Just get me where I can get my arm up above my head, where I can get my arm above my ear.* All the things that he said we would do, we did. Because of the relationship that was formed and the way he got to know me and love me, the challenges got easier.

Dodd tapped into something that I didn't even know I had inside of me. I had a bigger mission, something greater than myself. And there was no way that I would have been able to accomplish it without the team that God put around me. It was the ultimate change of mission mindset for me.

Stran's story is truly remarkable. He had to go through the crucibles of life so that he could form relationships with people like Dodd Romero, who knew him like no other, who cared for him like no other, not coddled but cared for him. Then Dodd was able to challenge him to achieve extraordinary elite results, which you'll read about later in this book.

Jeff Frye was a Major League Baseball player whose first day in the big leagues involved him getting called up from the AAA minor leagues. He got on a flight to the Dallas-Fort Worth Airport, where he was picked up in a taxi and driven to Arlington Stadium. As he rushed in and found his locker—his jersey was hanging there, ready for him, number 51—the locker room attendant looked at him and said, "You better check the lineup. You don't have time to take batting practice, but if you hurry, you can take some infield."

Frye dropped his gear and went over and checked the lineup. Sure enough, within hours of landing at the Dallas-Fort Worth Airport, Frye (a rookie) was playing second base for the Texas Rangers, with Nolan Ryan pitching. Jeff Frye's path to the major leagues is similar to Stran Smith's to a gold buckle, a remarkable journey and one I hope to get to tell one day.

However, it was a teammate of Frye's (aka "Frito") who, during a rain delay, helped him become a career .290 hitter. Frye was going through a slump and struggling with hitting. While waiting in the lobby of a hotel, as baseball players often do, Frye and a few of the other players filled time. As they goofed around with perhaps a wiffle ball bat or a broomstick, hitting a sock wrapped with tape, Frito started to imitate some of his favorite players.

One of the players that he imitated, Reuben Sierra, hit with a big leg kick, meaning he would lift his front left leg really high before he swung the bat. Frye was doing this imitation in the hotel lobby with teammate Rick Wrona. After throwing the sock ball several times and watching Jeff Frye simply crush it with this high leg kick, Rick Wrona said, "I know you're struggling right now. Why don't you hit like that in a game? With a leg kick?"

"You know what?" Frye said. "I think I will." Frye started to hit with a high leg kick. If you go back and look at his baseball cards online, you'll often see him hitting with a high leg kick. Now, if I had been walking through the hotel lobby before I knew Jeff personally and yelled, "Hey, Frito, hit like that in a game, dude!" Jeff would have thought I was some crackpot, crazy fan. He would have dismissed me. But Wrona knew Jeff, and he had cared for him; therefore, Jeff was willing to be challenged by his friend and teammate.

I play golf, fish, and hunt with Wrona and Frye often. We spend a lot of time together. We may joke with one another about this and that, but if anyone were to try and break into our circle without knowing and caring, they would not be taken seriously. If leaders, servers to a cause, want to be taken seriously and be respected, they need to apply the *Know, Care, Challenge* formula. It's what the 4% do.

Jeff Frye went on to hit nearly .300 over his career. He stands 5'8", and when he was called up to the majors, he weighed 165 pounds. Thanks to a friend who knew him, who had cared for him and challenged him to hit with a high leg kick, Jeff Frye came out of the slump. And later, with that high leg kick, Jeff Frye was one of only two players at the time to hit for the cycle for the Toronto Blue Jays, the other being Kelly Gruber.

KNOW, CARE, AND CHALLENGE THE PEOPLE YOU LEAD

Know, *Care*, and then *Challenge*. This secret formula of how the most elite operate and behave together is a great place for any leader, CEO, or coach to start. How well do you know your employees? How much have you cared for them? Sadly, most have it exactly the opposite. I *challenge* you (instruct), I pretend to *care* for you, and then I act like I *know* you and your spouse at the annual company Christmas party. Frankly, since leaving the Army in 2012, learning that most organizations behave this way broke my heart. I naively thought that they were better than that. Nope, most are average.

I have found that most organizations are loaded with hypocritical behaviors and poor morale. The situation is tolerated, and it shouldn't be. Among such organizations, there's typically a large personnel turnover rate (poor talent retention), and the named leader simply continues to *instruct* the newest members over and over again until they, too, leave. The more who leave, the more *instructive* the leader becomes. Why? It couldn't possibly be their failure as a leader. And no one will tell them. It also presents a HUGE opportunity for those organizations who invest in authentic leader development training and really take it seriously.

How well do you know the people you lead? So many times, when I work with a leader, they will present me with all the challenges that they have. I'll start to drill down and say, "Tell me about that employee, tell me about that player, tell me about that person."

"What do you mean?" they'll ask.

"Where are they from? What are their favorite things to do when they're not at work? Tell me about their family." All too often, the named leader can tell me very little about that so-called difficult employee.

Well, as General Magruder taught me years ago, when things go wrong, most of the time, if you start from your own position and work in concentric circles, you'll find a solution that is a lot closer to you than you may have even considered. Do you want a chance at leading an organization or leading in the six causes that Stran and I talk about—faith, family, friends, community, teams, and self? Apply the *Know, Care, Challenge* formula. That's what the elite do. It's not a guaranteed path to win, but it gives you the best opportunity.

As young boys and girls, when we got home from school, we were asked two very predictable questions: "How was your day?" and "Do you have any homework?" Keep in mind that from the day we are born, we have 18 or 19 Christmas trees before we leave the confines of the home or the family—however that is defined. And once we leave home, we will have spent 90% of the time (approximately) that we'll spend in an average lifetime with our families.

What's interesting about these two questions, "How was your day?" and "Do you have any homework?" They're the exact opposite of the questions that we should be asking. However, I was asked these questions, and I have caught myself and caught my wife asking our children those same predictable questions. It frustrates parents, but as Magruder said, start with yourself. As a 16-year-old boy, if I were ambushed with those questions, I would simply mumble back to my mom or dad, sometimes on purpose to frustrate my dad. It's not uncommon.

"How was your day?"

"Fine."

"Do you have any homework?"

"Uhhhh, I dunno."

The fact is, when your kids come home from school, they're tired, they're hungry, they have to go to the bathroom, and now they want to catch up on that thousand-dollar device, the smartphone (that phone belongs to your parents). We need to practice discipline, the subject of the later chapter, and not ambush them with those two predictable questions. We need to understand, to know, that they're tired, hungry, have to go to the bathroom, and want to catch up on their phone, and we need to tell them when we first see them after their long day at school, "I'm so glad to see you. Take a few minutes to go to the bathroom, get something to eat, catch your breath, and catch up on your phone. Then let's have a conversation."

By knowing their environment, empathizing with where they are in their lives, and demonstrating that we care about them, then, and only then, can we challenge them to have somewhat of a meaningful conversation.

But just listen to yourself during this school year. How many times will you ambush your children or even an employee with those questions? "How was your day? Do you have any homework?" Those two questions get you exactly nothing.

I see football coaches walk around as players are stretching before practice. They're patting them on the back. "Are you good? Are you good? You good?" Coach, they're not all doing "good." They may say they are. They're not. Get to know them.

Scan the QR code for bonus video content!

Bonus Video Content!

CHAPTER 6

Processes to Trust: The Decision-Making Process and the After-Action Review

"Trust the process."
–Nick Saban

• • •

BLUF: A real process is known. Team members can anticipate it. They can recite it. The elite require it.

• • •

To show you how important processes are, here's a hypothetical to consider: Suppose I told you that I knew the winning numbers for the lottery that night and that playing them was a guaranteed win. When I rattled them off to you, would you simply try to remember them, or would you take out a pen and a piece of paper and write them down? I don't know about y'all, but if I didn't have a pen, I'd scratch the numbers into my skin with a knife if I had to. Real processes are like that: they must be very intentional.

I've got notes written everywhere. I've got note cards. I've got notebooks. I've got records from 1995, when I started rodeoing—from all the rodeos I went to. I even have records from Odessa, Texas, the first rodeo I went to. I know what horse I rode in the first go-round, how much money I won, and how fast I was on that first calf.

Real processes require you to be very intentional about what you want to accomplish. Being a note-taker means you're not willing to leave anything to chance. You're a detailed person. I think that one of the first things—as a competitor, as a business owner, as an entrepreneur—is to be a person who has a real process and is very intentional.

Elite teams use two processes that include specific behaviors: the decision-making process (DMP) and the after-action review (AAR) process. Two questions I frequently ask when executive coaching are:
1. How do you make decisions, or what process do you use to make a decision?
2. How do you know if your decisions were right, or what process do you use to determine if you've made the right decision?

A simple search on the internet will give you an extraordinary amount of detail on both of these processes, more than we can share here. Here, we're simply going to cover them in a way that allows you to apply them immediately, whether it's in a business, to yourself, to an organization, or to a team, essentially across the six causes in your life.

DECISION-MAKING PROCESS (DMP)

The first process is the decision-making process. This process can be used for hasty decisions or a more strategic decision (long-term).

Mission: Your boss directs you to *buy a new car for the office.*

Step I: Intent: The decision maker states his or her INTENT. "We will buy a car in the next 30 days. Staff, come up with a plan." It must be clearly stated and written down. Once the intent is communicated, it's repeated back to the decision maker to ensure that it has been properly understood by the people it has been communicated to.

Step II: Guidance: The decision-maker provides screening criteria to further describe their intent: a budget of $40K, a new gas car, four doors, any type of interior (cloth or leather), and a minimum of 25 MPG.

Step III: Assumptions and Facts: The staff makes some valid assumptions and states facts.
- We have $40K.
- The color of the car doesn't matter (not mentioned).
- There's a new car available within a hundred miles.
- We only have 20 days to look (because of various schedules).

Step IV: Courses of Actions (COAs): Three options are developed, and an in-progress review, or IPR, is scheduled. Remember, the decision hasn't been made yet. The IPR is a cross-check. Are we on the right path? Are the three options valid? Are the assumptions valid? Are the facts true? Is there any *new* information or guidance?
- Car A, Car B, Car C
- List three advantages and three disadvantages for each option that meets the screening criteria.

Step V: In-Progress Review (IPR): Staff meets with the decision maker, who restates their intent and checks to see if there is any new information. Doing an IPR is a must. It keeps things from going sideways and discovers blind spots or new information.
- The staff learns during the IPR that the budget is now $45K, not $40K, and the car must be red. (Why red? The staff doesn't care. They're curious, but they don't care.)

Step VI: More COA Development: The staff adjusts the options (COAs) and schedules a decision meeting. At the meeting, they present three options, along with the advantages and disadvantages of each and make a recommendation on which car to buy. Then the decision maker decides which option to go with.

- Car A, Car B, or Car C. The decision maker chooses Car C, which is the one the staff recommended. He may, however, decide he wants Car B. The staff shouldn't care. The decision-making process (DMP) drives an objective outcome. The company buys Car C. That's the decision, and it was an outcome of the process.

At times, the advantages and disadvantages of each of the options are given weights or values (I use a scale from one to five). For example, a high school graduate deciding on what college to attend may include "close to home" as being vitally important, a valued advantage (five points).

We hosted the National Collegiate Boxing Championships at West Point. I was the decision maker for how the event would operate. During the IPR, I was briefed on the plan—we had three weeks before the event. The plan was OK, but it wasn't what I envisioned. I stated at the IPR, "We are not thinking big enough." Then, I described what I expected regarding food and beverage, a silent auction, seating, lighting, etc. I gave a clearer and more detailed INTENT. Had we not conducted an IPR, the staff's performance would have been average at best. They were given permission to innovate/create/execute at the IPR. Schedule IPRs. The event was epic (and we beat Navy, again!). We were asked to host it again the following year.

The decision maker must communicate very clearly what their intent is (Step I). As Stran mentioned, it should be written down. What's interesting about the DMP is what occurs *after* the decision is made.

After a decision is made, for organizations that do NOT have a process, members stand up, leave the room, meet in their little tribes—in their break room or hallways, back at the cubicles, or in position group meetings (football coaches)—and begin to undermine/question the decision. They may say things like, "I can't believe that decision was made. A red car? A RED car? That's the decision? This will never work. I hate red cars. Wait till they see the outcome of this decision."

The elite, however, "trust the process," so much so that when the decision maker decides, they all rise as one. They know the work has been done, an objective process was used, and a decision was made for the cause. Each member of that team owns that decision as if they had made it themselves.

When they return to their subordinate units or teams, they are not overly excited but *objectively and fully committed* to the decision. They speak in the first person, saying, "Here's what we are doing," and the members of those subordinate teams say, "Okay, let's execute."

They also know that an after-action review (AAR), another process that we will cover here, will determine if the correct decision was made. They trust that process as well. You see, real processes are never personal. They are all about the cause, the mission, the vision, the values, and trusting the leader's intention to be authentic, relentless, and selfless. Real processes are never personal or emotional. They're objective and committed to the cause. The behaviors associated with the decision-making process are where the magic happens.

AFTER-ACTION REVIEW (AAR) PROCESS

In the Navy, it's called a "hot wash." Businesses often refer to it as "lessons learned." After every *major* decision in our military is made, an AAR is *immediately* scheduled. What's important about the AAR process is that, unlike the decision-making process, power must be removed from the room or the discussion.

The colonel or the boss must sit among the members of the team or the soldiers. An AAR must be facilitated by someone who is not in a position of power; otherwise, the truth will not evolve. Therefore, the leader must be humble enough to sit among the ranks and listen to the truth.

The after-action review process usually answers the following four questions:
1. What did we set out to do?
2. What actually happened (the truth)?
3. What do we want to improve or sustain? This is often written in green.
4. What do we want to eliminate or improve? This is often written in red.

Then, a discussion occurs with some guidelines:
1. Everyone must have thick skin.
2. Everyone must participate.
3. No egos, no rank.

This is about the cause, the mission—not any individual. The most elite leaders that I've ever met, including General Magruder, always want to get to the truth. They don't care if they are wrong or made a mistake. It's not about the CEO. It's not about the president or head coach. It's about the team, the organization, the family. The willingness of leaders to be vulnerable and hear the truth from members of the team is vital for the after-action review process, whether it's after a school year, fiscal year, rodeo, or football game.

The AAR process is often overlooked—most corporate or athletics departments do not do it. This means that the organizations that do schedule them have a huge advantage over the ones that don't. I worked with a large bank and insurance company in Houston. The CEO stated, "The end-of-year

AAR is the most important thing we do all year." It's how they get better, and they are very good. Since the CEO stood up and stated this in front of everyone, the AAR session went very well.

After a big football game, what do coaches sometimes say or do? I was in one football staff meeting in the NCAA (a Power Five school) after an unexpected mid-season loss. This was a game they actually paid the opponent to play. It's called a "guarantee game," meaning the home team is most likely to win. The truth is the only thing that's *guaranteed* is that the check written to the opponent will clear the bank. In this case, the home team lost, and it was national news.

The next day, everyone on the team shrugged and said, "We had a bad game. We made a lot of mental mistakes. We went left and should have gone right. We never got any good calls. Injuries, bad night, bad officiating. We were due to lose. We were tired. We had an illness on the team. The third-string quarterback couldn't execute. Okay, what does everybody want to do?" I even heard a coach say, "Just burn the tape (the video). Let's get ready for the next opponent."

I later discovered that at this high-level academic university, the week of that particular "guarantee" game included an unusually HIGH academic load: tests, papers, projects, and midterms. The coaches never realized it (blind spot). They didn't have a process. The next year, with a new coaching staff, guess what happened? They lost the same week again because of the same reasons. I suspect they still don't know why.

There was no process. There was no willingness, no humility from the head coach to conduct an AAR. No one asked, "What did we set out to do? What exactly happened—the truth? What do we want to improve or sustain? What do we want to eliminate?"

The beauty of an AAR is that it creates a historical document. I sat in an NCAA football head coach's staff meeting in the Southeastern Conference (SEC) a few years ago (not in Texas). As the spring football game was being discussed, the head coach asked, "What did we do last year?" Silence. "What uniforms did we wear?" Silence. "We're going to have 20,000 fans in the stands for our spring game Saturday. Does anyone remember what we did last year?" Again, nothing. "How many plays did we run?" You get the idea.

Had they *scheduled* and conducted an AAR after the spring game the year prior, they could have easily pulled up the AAR document on the big screen for all to see and come up with a plan to better execute this year's event. They had nothing to refer to other than a couple of coaches who were still there who remembered bits and pieces of the game. There was no "process TO trust." The head coach was earning millions of dollars a year.

Trust the process? What process? The DMP and the AAR. They are used by the elite all the time.

Sometimes, they are formal processes that take days, but other times, they're hasty. They're five minutes, ten minutes. Often, before the elite close their eyes at night, they'll say to themselves, "What did I set out to do today? What actually happened? The truth. What do I want to improve? What do I want to sustain?" The answers don't have to be complicated. They don't have to be long, but they do have to be determined. Hard work is not a process; that's expected. Every major event needs an AAR. With three daughters, you can bet we've had three AARs for two weddings, with one more to go (one of the reasons I'm writing a book, lol).

The reason the Colonel and I wrote this book is that we don't feel like we ever arrived. It's not enough to be a great player, win a World Championship, or build a successful business if that's as far as it goes. These principles are meant to provide you with the tools to be elite in every aspect of your life.

Personally, I've never had a problem using the three courses of action and then doing the after-action review. At this stage of my life, the challenge for me is seeing my children run into problems. When they run into a wall, the first thing I want to do is help them. I know how to get over that wall. I can show you. Let me climb that wall, and I'll pull you up and show you how to do this. The hardest thing for me is to stand back and watch them struggle and claw to get over that wall. I have to be there for them but not do it for them. For their development and journey to become elite, I have to allow them to climb most walls on their own.

I've climbed a few walls in my life, and I was able to get over some of them, and some of them, I didn't. But it was the struggle that developed me the most. It goes against our instincts to allow them to struggle, but we have to remember that the point is not to get to the top of that wall; it's to get to the other side.

See, that's where we mess up a lot. We struggle, we climb, we claw, and we get to the top. Then, when we get on top of that wall, we want to pound our chests and say, "Look at me! I'm king of the mountain!" No, that's not the goal. The goal is to climb down to the other side and get grounded. The Colonel talks a lot about being grounded. It's very important. That's the end of everything: get grounded and take your shoes off. Whenever you climb that wall and get back down on the other side, get grounded.

Once you're grounded, it's time for the after-action review. It's time to talk about the lessons learned. I want to be there as a dad for every step of this, but I think it's critical that you let that employee, young person, son, or daughter climb that wall themselves. Encourage them and get on the other side. Don't stand on top of the mountain. Get grounded, and then have your after-action review.

The idea of peer reviews panics most, but they are just another tool to remain aligned with the necessary behaviors to operate and function at an elite level. Whenever I work with a college football team, for example, the moment I mention the idea of peer reviews, they start thinking they're going to have to "rat" one another out. In the case of a corporation, they start thinking about HR and the problems associated with peer reviews. Those are all excuses.

As you're reading this, you may be thinking peer reviews must be used to get rid of somebody. That's not the case at all. The elite use peer reviews as a developmental tool, not a punitive one, to ensure that every member of the team is aligned and committed to serving the cause, mission, vision, and values. They're never personal. They never violate HR rules, and they never require ratting out a teammate. They're developmental.

The challenge with introducing peer reviews to a corporation, business, or athletics team is they only do it once. If you want true development, they have to be scheduled at least twice a year. Organizations that are committed to becoming elite are unafraid to schedule peer reviews. I work with those organizations to develop objective reviews that often involve three nominative questions and two narratives. Here's an example of a peer review:

Question 1: Among your peers (a position group in sports), who is the most trustworthy?

Question 2: Who is the person who serves/leads our team relentlessly?

Question 3: Where do you place your day-to-day behavior among your peers? Top 10%, Top 30%, Top 50% or Bottom 50%?

Narrative Question 1: "What is one thing we are doing that we should continue to do?"

Narrative Question 2: "What is one thing we're not currently doing that we should consider?"

Imagine scheduling such a review every quarter or twice a year and committing to that process. Many times, peer reviews reveal blind spots. For example, as a coaching staff for the 2004-2005 Army West Point Baseball team, we thought we knew exactly who the leaders were on our team. However, peer reviews revealed that the team identified our bullpen catcher as the most selfless, relentless, and authentic player on our roster. We knew he was fully committed. We had no idea what he was doing for the team away from the practice field (tutoring his classmates, making sure they made all their treatments, etc.). A player that was never going to start in a conference game was the player the team respected and loved the most. We named him one of our captains. He's still on active duty. His name is Tommy Halverson. In my view, he was one of our MVPs during that record-setting season (when we swept Navy 4-0).

Do you know why most leaders won't conduct peer reviews?—fear of discovery, a lack of humility, or the presence of ego. Peer reviews are a vital part of a process. Among the elite, once peer reviews are scheduled, they are rarely rescheduled or canceled. Why? The moment they are postponed or rescheduled, their importance has been cheapened. If they are non-negotiable, it sends a message: "This is important. This is how we will win consistently. Trust the process."

Scan the QR code for bonus video content!

Bonus Video Content!

CHAPTER 7

Doing Discipline

"Make us to choose the harder right instead of the easier wrong..."
−West Point Cadet Prayer

"When things go wrong, start from your own position and look in concentric circles. You'll often find that a solution to your problem is a lot closer to you than you thought."
−Lieutenant General Lawson W. Magruder III

• ● •

BLUF: Discipline is not a choice for the elite. It's a requirement.

• ● •

For this chapter, we're going to look at several examples of discipline. It might surprise you that discipline exists in places you may not have considered: in athletics, in business, after a setback, at home, while fly-fishing, obviously in our military, with our diet, how we work, and how we think.

Many people are familiar with the documentary *The Last Dance*, the story of the Chicago Bulls and how their struggles with the Detroit Pistons continued year after year until they did not. It had several parts that I was curious about, specifically with players like Dennis Rodman and Scottie

Pippen. However, when I watch a documentary like that, there's always one moment that stands out. This time, it was the Bulls' last loss to the Pistons in the NBA playoffs.

The game was over, and the Bulls had been eliminated from the playoffs again. The camera focused on Michael Jordan getting dressed after another devastating loss. He was putting on a khaki suit and lacing up his shoes. Then he looked up at his trainer and said, "We start tomorrow."

At that point, it was over for everybody else. Michael Jordan was about to do what Stran Smith needed to do to become a world champion: "We start tomorrow."

The very next morning, Michael Jordan changed everything about his approach to practice, rest, sleep, nutrition, his thoughts, and even how he engaged in the press. He started tomorrow. That's one example of discipline. His *intentions* no longer mattered; only his *actions* did.

Another great documentary is *The Greatest Night in Pop Music*, about how Lionel Richie led a talented and diverse group of musicians to record what is thought by many to be one of the most remarkable songs in history: "We Are The World." When I do executive coaching, I often start by requiring staff and leaders to watch *The Greatest Night in Pop Music* and how Lionel Richie had to practice extraordinary discipline when dealing with a plethora of different personalities, countless distractions, and fatigue.

Lionel Richie was able to do discipline at a time when the average leader simply hadn't even considered it. He had a mission (a vision). He could see that what they were doing in those incredibly challenging conditions at three and four o'clock in the morning was going to be worth it. He was tired (he hadn't been up for five days like Stran, but he was smoked). The song had to be recorded in a specific amount of time. It was only going to happen if he had the discipline to adapt to each and every personality in that room. It was a remarkable leadership laboratory.

I've never met Lionel Richie or Michael Jordan, but some of the things I witnessed in those documentaries indicate to me that they have the behaviors and attributes that put them among the top 4%.

DISCIPLINED THOUGHT PRECEDES ACTION

Most every father or "man" of the house, perhaps even a grandfather, has their own chair where they sit. And with that chair comes a predictable routine. If my father-in-law walked into the room and one of us was sitting in his chair, the implied task was to stop what we were doing and find another chair. He didn't need to say a word.

Depending on your age, you may have some reading glasses hanging on a nearby lamp, a place where you put your coffee mug or favorite beverage, or a magazine that you're reading. For me, it's *Texas Parks and Wildlife*. For so many others, it could be a book that they're reading (*A Colonel & A Cowboy*). And in *my* particular chair in *my* office, there's a place where I keep the remote control. It's on the right arm of the chair. There have been times, though, when I've sat in *my* chair, grabbed *my* reading glasses and the latest issue of *Texas Parks and Wildlife*, took a sip of a cold cup of coffee, and reached for the remote control only to discover that it was not there.

Without doing disciplined thought, I immediately get frustrated. I start to stack my amygdala. I've seen myself do this, where I will say in a loud voice with an irritated tone, "Girls, who took the remote control? Who took the clicker?" And immediately, one of our daughters will start blaming the other one, saying she took it and removed the battery so she could play a video game. You get the idea. I have created chaos among our three daughters because I was not situationally aware or self-aware and did not do discipline.

Discipline, an action, is preceded by a thought. Please read that again. It starts with a thought. Had I done discipline—had I been situationally aware and self-aware and then taken action—I would have realized that when I sat in *my* chair (pronouns are important, I've heard...) I knocked the remote control off the arm, and it was now lying between the arm and the cushion.

"Never mind, girls. Your *heroic* father has found the remote control." At that point, it doesn't matter to the girls; I've disrupted them. They've now moved on to arguing about other events—their amygdalas are now hijacked. I've hijacked the whole family! We're all jacked up. They're arguing about clothes and hair brushes upstairs. Why? Because I did not do discipline from my own position. I caused the problem, and then I acted like I solved the problem that I created (politicians do this all the time). Doing discipline at home matters. Let's look at another inspirational example of discipline.

DOING DISCIPLINE

Ben Hunt Davis, a remarkable man and athlete, competed in the 1992 Barcelona Games and the 1996 Atlanta Olympic Games and won a silver medal in 1999 in the rowing championships. The British hadn't won a gold medal in rowing since 1912. Like Michael Jordan, Ben Hunt Davis was fed up with finishing second. He was by himself when he did discipline (which, in my experience, is THE most important time to do it—alone).

The day after they lost the gold medal in 1999, he woke up and said, "From this moment on until the 2000 Olympics, everything that I'm going to do in my life will center around one question: *will it make the boat go faster?*" His thoughts, his actions, his personal relationships, how he treated equipment, and how he treated teammates were driven by one question: will this make the boat go faster? In the 2000 Summer Olympics in Sydney, Australia, Ben Hunt Davis led his rowing team to Britain's first gold medal in the sport since 1912. It's a remarkable story, one worth looking up.

I played junior college baseball with some remarkably talented players, one of whom was Jimmy Morris, who was played by Dennis Quaid in the movie *The Rookie*. Incidentally, the real Jimmy Morris looks nothing like Dennis Quaid.

But another player I had the privilege of knowing who's stayed in my life as a dear friend is Ellis Burks. Ellis was the first 20-20 man for the Boston Red Sox, the first to steal 20 bases and hit 20 home runs in a single season. Ellis and I were both 17-year-old freshmen at Ranger Junior College, and he and I connected early on. He was the first person to beat me in the 60-yard dash, and I'll never forget it. As he passed me, his ball cap blew off his head, and the brim of his hat hit me in the lip! When we finished, he looked at me and said, "Damn, you're a fast little mother frog." Not as fast as him. In 1988, Bo Jackson was the only player in the majors who could beat Ellis Burks to first base. There's some context.

Ellis is from Everman, Texas. Everything he did in junior college was centered on getting him to the major leagues. He promised his grandmother at the hospital that he would go to college, but he was fully committed (not just interested) to making it to the major leagues. Believe it or not, in Ranger, Texas, it gets very cold during the winter. Ellis realized that no matter how cold it was or what time of morning it was, he could knock on my door, and I would answer. Ellis would wake me up early on freezing winter weekend mornings and tell me, "We need to go hit."

The two of us would go out to a dilapidated batting cage with torn nets and baseballs that were ripped open and needed to be taped, and he would put on two sets of torn-up batting gloves—sometimes, they'd be winter gloves and not made for hitting a baseball. For hours, I would throw to him, and he would hit the ball over and over again. It was painfully cold, but it was just the two of us out there.

The cages that we hit in, the batting cages in junior college, were nothing like what Division I baseball programs have today. These cages were dangerous. There were holes in the net and not very much protection. Countless times, the baseball would come off of Ellis's aluminum bat and hit me in the shoulder or glance off my knee. But Ellis and I did this time and time again.

One particular day, he had hit for so long, and his hands were so cold that his fingers cracked and bled. I thought about that bitterly cold day in July 1987. I was a lieutenant in the Army, seated in a tapioca field in Thailand on a sweltering, 107-degree day, and someone brought me *The Stars and Stripes* newspaper. I always read the newspaper from the back page to the front because I wanted to read the sports section first and I am also left-handed. There, I read that the Boston Red Sox had called up "rookie sensation" Ellis Burks.

Ellis was fully committed. I don't know what he would have done if he hadn't made the majors. In 2004, when the Boston Red Sox won the World Series, Ellis had three baseballs signed by the entire Red Sox roster. He gave one to his father, kept one for himself, and sent one to me. Ellis has never forgotten those countless hours the two of us spent in extraordinarily difficult conditions, doing discipline.

On a recent fly-fishing trip to Cody, Wyoming, I became very, very frustrated. I could not tie the knots required to fly fish. In fact, I was wasting a lot of time getting frustrated on the banks of the Shoshone River. It was really irritating me, and then I realized I had not done the discipline of learning to tie knots. So, when we went back to our cabin, just outside of Cody, I spent two hours learning how to tie knots. Yes, I went on YouTube, found a video on the subject, and studied the fundamentals of knot tying. Then, for the next hour, I just simply tied knots over and over and over again.

The next day, I had a much more productive time, but I had not earned the right to catch fish because I had not put in the work. I hadn't repped it. What the hell did I expect? I had only learned how to tie the knots, but I thought I would just go out there and catch fish. Discipline comes in many forms.

PARENTING WITH DISCIPLINE

What about parents doing discipline? By that, I don't mean disciplining their children; I mean it in another way. Let them experience and figure stuff out without being rescued from a minor setback. Our 12-year-old daughter approached me one day and said, "Dad, I've got this great project I'm doing at school, but it's going to require me to go to Hobby Lobby to buy some materials. Will you go with me?" Of course, I said yes.

She showed me the list of items she needed to get, and I noticed that it was rather long. I asked her how much money she had saved. She had about $15 with her, but as I looked at her list, I could pretty well calculate that if she was going to buy everything on it, it was going to be well over that amount. So, I decided to make the Hobby Lobby a leadership laboratory. However, I knew that it was going to require discipline on my part as her father.

So, off to Hobby Lobby we went, and I explained to her, "Now, listen. If you get to the checkout counter and everything you have in your basket ends up costing more than the money you have in your pocket, Daddy's going to be standing outside, and I am not going to go in and pay for the amount that you need to get all the things on your list. You're going to have to make some decisions on how to get within your budget.

"Oh," she said. "Okay, Daddy. I understand."

When we got there, she went into Hobby Lobby and spent the next 15 minutes gathering up all the articles on her list. Then, when she got to the checkout counter, she realized she did not have enough money. Behind her were four or five ladies who were very serious about their hobbies, and they became very frustrated with this girl who did not have enough money to pay for the items in her basket. I watched all of this through the glass windows.

My heart was racing, and I could easily have gone in and rescued her from this moment. But this needed to be a crucible for our daughter, a leadership laboratory. I could see her getting frustrated, and I saw her motion to the cashier to wait one second. Then she ran outside the building and said, "Daddy, I understand, I understand. All I need is five more dollars. Can you please give it to me?" At that moment, I had to be disciplined.

I took a deep breath and said, "Sweetheart, you're going to have to go back in there and deal with this issue. I have the money in my pocket, but it's not about the money. This is about you going through the process of understanding."

She went back in and dealt with the issue. As difficult as it was, it certainly was not life-threatening, but to this day, she talks about that. As a 30-year-old, married, successful businesswoman in Austin, Texas, our daughter still talks about the time when her father had to be disciplined, and that allowed her to go through one of life's little crucibles at the age of 12.

When Yankees owner George Steinbrenner was alive, he paid for the entire Army West Point baseball team to train with the New York Yankees for 12 days every spring break. He did not want the press to know about this. He did not want articles written about this, but for 10 to 12 days, the Army West Point baseball team traveled to Florida to train with the New York Yankees.

I was an assistant baseball coach for that remarkable team. We got beat by Florida State 3–2 on a home-cooked call that I'm still not over. And I repeat—I'm required by law to tell the readers that we did sweep Navy that year, four games. Well, when we were training with the New York Yankees one particular day, we finished about 15 minutes early. There were four baseball fields, like a four-leaf clover, and I decided, as a non-salary assistant baseball coach, the only active-duty officer on the coaching staff, that I would go over and watch the single-leg New York Yankees practice for a few minutes. I was astounded at what I witnessed. About 11 players were standing at home plate. They were not holding a bat, and there was no pitcher. There was a coach at first base, a coach at third base, and a coach standing at home plate.

The coach at home plate said, "Gentlemen, today we are going to practice home run trots." The players, who were around 18 or 19 years old, giggled at that. The coach continued, "Gentlemen, you are New York Yankees. You are members of an organization that has won 27 World Championships. We are not here to showboat. We are not here to insult worthy opponents. We brought you here because we believe, one day, you're going to hit a home run for the New York Yankees, and when you do, this is how you behave. You're going to take a shadow swing without a bat or a ball, and then you're going to run the bases."

You can imagine how underdeveloped the prefrontal cortexes were of the young men standing behind home plate. The coach was teaching them the discipline of behavior. The first time, they clowned around in the batter's box and made some dramatic swings. But then the coach stood behind the pitcher's mound and talked to them as they rounded the bases.

"You're a New York Yankee. You just did what we expected you to do. Touch all the bases, shake the first base coach's hand and the third base coach's hand. Touch all the bases and home plate and get back in the dugout to celebrate, mentally grounded and with your teammates." I watched in awe as they did this three times. By the third time, these young men took this little exercise of running the bases as if they had hit a home run very seriously. They were training discipline, the discipline of behavior.

As I mentioned earlier, Colonel Eric Kail and I served together at West Point. One night, his son came in an hour and a half after curfew. He had clearly been out way too late, probably doing things that he should not have been doing.

At that moment Eric's amygdala could have easily been hijacked as a father who was infuriated that his son was an hour and a half late. Then, he realized that now was not the time to instill punitive measures. Eric had to do discipline. He shared this with me because he knew I had daughters and, one day, they would be late as well and break curfew. He said, "The best way to handle a situation like that is when that son or daughter walks through the front door late. When you are emotional, mad, upset, and worried, that is the time you must be disciplined and say, 'I'm so glad to see you. I'm grateful you are alive and home. Let's get some rest, and tomorrow morning, let's have a discussion. I want to hear your plan.'" The next morning, his son punished himself more harshly than Eric would have.

I've talked about General Magruder. Every morning at 5 a.m., I would drive by then-Colonel Magruder's office in a Volkswagen Bug convertible, blue with a white top. I wanted to confirm that he was truly the authentic, relentless, and selfless leader that I believed he was, so I would glance to my right, and there he would be, working away with the light on at his desk. He was in charge of 1,500–2,000 soldiers. Every morning, he would do the discipline of handwriting a note to at least one of them. He was repping character. And it was the right thing to do.

Discipline comes in many forms, such as our thoughts, situational awareness, and self-awareness, but for those who truly are fully committed to winning, discipline is not a choice; it is a requirement.

In December 2004, after the tenth go-round at the National Finals Rodeo, I was walking down the tunnel on the ground floor of the Thomas & Mack Center feeling exhausted and heartbroken and fighting back the tears for a year that was almost, but not quite. I crossed paths with an employee from the Professional Rodeo Cowboys Association (PRCA), and as he walked by, he said, "Oh, hey, Stran."

As I turned back to respond to him, he pitched me a case. "Almost forgot," he said nonchalantly. In that little cardboard box was a buckle: the tenth go-round buckle. In the National Finals, winning one of those buckles is usually one of the most celebrated things you can do. When you win a go-round, you usually go over to the Gold Coast Casino (now the South Point Casino), and they bring you and your family up on stage. You talk about your run that night, and it's the highlight of that night. You beat the other 14 competitors.

On the tenth go-round, however, after they hand out the World Championship, there's no fanfare for the go-round winner. No celebration, no stage with a cheering crowd. No, they just toss that go-round buckle to you like it's an afterthought. The only one celebrating after the tenth round is the world champion. I had just lost a World Championship by less than fifteen hundred dollars. At that point, you'd almost have to think the money is down the drain because my total and only goal was to win a World Championship. My heart broken, I thought, *I will never let it come down this way again.*

Right then, I knew that all the all-night practices, the blood, sweat, and tears, the driving, the pain, the injuries, fighting back, the rehab, and spending hours on my own in the rehab facilities, gym, and practice pen would lead to a 3% improvement so that I was never in this position again, second in the world. At that point, I adopted the phrase, "Whatever you do regularly will determine what you will eventually have."

I didn't know, as you've read in the first chapter, what was to come: I was going to lose the greatest horse that had ever lived and would have to transform my body and my entire philosophy of rodeo. The way I did it, the way I practiced, the way I prepared, everything would have to turn on its ear for this 3% increase. We'll tell the rest of this story and what happened in 2008 later in the book.

TIME + KNOWLEDGE/INSTRUCTION = UNDERSTANDING

Being disciplined?

Discipline is a remarkable attribute that everyone has the opportunity to put into play in their lives. Doing discipline does not guarantee that one will become a member of the 4% elite, but it is a requirement. Kevin O'Leary, known as "Mr. Wonderful" on *Shark Tank*, said in a recent podcast interview, "I will not hire workaholics. They work very hard, but they do not have the discipline required to maintain their maximum capacity to sleep, to recover, to heal, to have other interests. I look for people who have discipline when it comes to work but also have other interests and disciplines that will allow them to be either more innovative, creative, and productive at work."

You see, being a workaholic is not a process. Being a workaholic is not discipline. However, discipline is a requirement for becoming elite. We'll explore other examples of discipline as we move through this book, but for now, I'll leave you with this: What is your first response to a setback, injury, loss, or pain?

It would be unrealistic to say that we do not acknowledge it. Even the elite briefly acknowledge setbacks, pain, and loss. Then they take a deep breath and anchor to the one non-negotiable requirement: doing discipline and moving on. Change of Mission.

You can imagine my reaction when I walked into that leadership football academy over a decade ago and heard this colonel say that only 4% make the elite. When I heard this, and I knew that I had done everything that I had done for a 3% increase, I realized that it was about the details. I knew that this man could speak to me in a way that I understood, and that, I believe, was the beginning of our relationship.

Scan the QR code for bonus video content!

Bonus Video Content!

CHAPTER 8

How We Learn

*"Our most favorite coaches, teachers and mentors knew
how to reach us. Our least favorite never did."*
–J. Craig Flowers

• • •

**BLUF: If you are a named leader who wonders how to become
more effective, start with *Know, Care,* then *Challenge*. However,
understand that *Knowing* involves figuring out HOW one best
learns and develops. Leaders adapt to the ones they
are called to lead.**

• • •

One of the most fascinating things that I've had the privilege of being a part of is studying the science and training of human behavior in support of some elite organizations. I was also trained in the art/science of pedagogy as an assistant professor at West Point, an accredited four-year university. I got a chance to apply what I learned directly to the fields of friendly strife, as MacArthur said, as an NCAA Division I assistant baseball coach (we swept Navy, btw). It was a fascinating seat in which I had the privilege to learn exactly how humans learned and developed.

People learn and develop in three different arenas. The first is in the classroom, through note-taking, lectures, and film study. The second is individual learning: doing homework, reading, studying playbooks or the employee handbook. And the final arena is hands-on learning or doing.

The challenge for leaders, whether you're a business leader, parent, cowboy, or athlete, is to discover how each person learns and develops and then adapt how information and instructions are delivered to them. Stran Smith had two main people on his team: his wife, Jennifer, and Dodd Romero. These two people knew Stran, cared for him, and were able to challenge him (a formula we covered earlier in this book) in the best way for him to receive it. Dodd and Jennifer know Stran well enough to know how he best absorbs information and knowledge. Most leaders, teachers, and coaches, however, only deliver instructions and information in the manner in which *they* best learn, and that is a huge blind spot. They may not even realize that they do this.

At the NFL Combine, I was sitting with Bill Polian, a Hall of Fame former general manager. We spent about 30 to 45 minutes together, one-on-one, and I'd been to the NFL Combine three or four times. As I talked about how humans learn and how it could potentially be used as a competitive edge in the NFL Draft, Bill sat back and listened carefully, and then he scratched his head. He had just purchased a hat for his grandson, and I could tell he was ready to leave our meeting. He said, "Colonel, despite all the testing that we do, the Wunderlich tests, all the interviews, all the physical measurements, and the skill exams… despite all that analysis, we are lucky if we get it right half the time."

To put that into perspective, the NFL is on a path to becoming a $20 billion industry, and they still don't do better than flipping a coin when it comes to hiring (drafting) talent. The biggest threat to an organization like the NFL, as is the case with most organizations, is ego. Coaches love to say, "Coaching is teaching, and teaching is coaching." I've heard it all the time in high school, college, and the NFL.

But when I ask them, "Okay, Coach, what is your teaching philosophy?" I get a blank stare.

THREE VERY DIFFERENT LEARNERS

The art of teaching is lost in coaching and business. You can't tell an NCAA or NFL head coach that, though—he won't believe you. Ego. Some will accept it, but most won't. There's no better example of this than to look at three different players who happen to play for the same university: Ricky Williams, Heisman Trophy winner for the University of Texas, David Thomas out of Lubbock, Texas, who was a tight end for the same university, and, of course, the great Vince Young, who won a national championship at the position of quarterback for the Longhorns. Each of those players learned very differently.

Ricky Williams, for example, learned only by doing. He had to be on the field (roping the calf), running the football, to understand and learn the playbook the way he needed to. In fact, after EVERY play in practice, Ricky would run the ball all the way to the end zone so he could imagine turning the play into a touchdown. It drove his coaches nuts. He did this every play. Sitting in a classroom and going to meetings were wastes of Ricky's elite talent and time.

I know how these three players learn because, in 2012, along with Eric Kail and a few others including former TCU teammate Lew Williams, I helped build and launch an interactive assessment tool called APTUS Discovery. We measured exactly how a person defined, processed, and executed instructions and information in a fraction of a second using an interactive set of ten video exercises on a tablet (the assessment took 30 minutes and delivered a blueprint to HOW to best reach and teach players). We assessed these three players, and I read their unique Bottom Line Up Front (BLUF) Reports LIVE on the set of *Longhorn Game Day* on a Saturday night. All three were blown away by how accurate we were.

David Thomas (DT) is a personal friend now. David, we discovered, learns best through individual study (homework), in this case, the New Orleans Saints' playbook. I've roomed with him on the road doing football camps, and every night and morning, DT reads. When DT was traded from the Patriots to the Saints, he was picked up at the airport, and on the ride over to the New Orleans Saints practice facility, he was told, "We didn't trade for you to play in two weeks. We traded for you to play this Sunday." Then, they handed him his playbook.

That night, he devoured it from cover to cover—similar to how Stran and I hope you're devouring this book. DT studied the playbook in precise detail. With only a handful of physical practices on the field, they were *unable* to walk through every play prior to his first game as a Saint. On one particular play, DT was the fourth choice as a receiver, meaning that if quarterback Drew Brees decided that the first, second, and third receivers were not open, David would suddenly become the number-one receiver. He would be what's called "hot," only if the safety and the linebacker both blitzed. The term "hot" means all bets are off; we are throwing you (DT) the football. The implied task is—be ready.

DT had never practiced this play, but he had read about it. The play was called in the huddle, and then David went to the line of scrimmage. When the ball was snapped, he noticed out of the corner of his right eye that the safety and the linebacker were blitzing. He told me that he thought, *I remember this in the playbook (remember: a thought occurs before an action). If those two guys blitz, I think I become...* and before he could finish the thought, he turned his head with his hands in a catching position near his facemask, and boom! Drew Brees delivered the football. That was DT's first catch as a New Orleans Saint. They later went on to win the Super Bowl. David Thomas learned predominantly by individual study and by doing his homework. Vince Young, on the other hand, learned not only by doing but by film study (in the classroom).

I spent time with Vince Young, and he confirmed to me that David Thomas was one of his favorite targets at the University of Texas. They would stay late and often take extra physical reps together. But Vince Young would devour film study. He wanted to know exactly what a play looked like so he could go out and execute it like no other.

Each of these three players had different experiences in the National Football League. Why? Because they had different coaches. David Thomas had two coaches, Bill Belichick (New England Patriots) and Sean Payton (Saints). They understood David, knew him, cared about him, and could challenge him. The other two players had very different experiences in the NFL, some of which were very frustrating—in large part because the coaches did not know how to best reach and teach them. Ricky Williams learned best by doing, David Thomas by individual study, and Vince Young by doing and classroom (film study).

It's one of the reasons why I tell people to watch *The Greatest Night of Pop Music*. Specifically, watch how Lionel Richie and Stevie Wonder were able to reach an introverted, shy, and lost Bob Dylan (who wanted to serve the cause). If you've seen this show, you'll see that it wasn't until Stevie Wonder modeled what Bob Dylan should do that Dylan felt comfortable enough doing it live and recording the song. Stevie Wonder had figured out how to reach Dylan, and he did it without sight. It's a remarkable scene.

It's very frustrating to me when I hear coaches at the highest level deliver instructions and information in a classroom setting or even on the field. At the end of their remarks, they'll rather loudly say, "Does that make sense?" In fact, they often shorten it to "Make sense?" No student or player in the history of education or football has ever raised their hand and said, "No, that doesn't make sense." If you have a player or student who learns like Ricky Williams did with a hands-on approach, there's no way he's going to raise his hand and say that he doesn't understand. Instead, that star talent is going to go out to the field, get in the back of the line, and wait for someone else to model it before he steps up.

A coach will often get frustrated by this, thinking that the most talented player should go first, but when the player does, he goes left when he should have gone right. Then the coach will rip him a new one in front of so-called "family members" (teammates), having hung signs on walls for recruits to see, claiming that they're "family" here. I've been to a lot of college practices at the highest levels (in the SEC, where it just *costs* more), and I've heard how some of these coaches talk to players. I can't imagine talking to a family member that way. The fact is, they don't know their players, and they haven't cared for them. They only know how to challenge them. They have it exactly wrong.

THE SUCCESSFUL COACH

Understanding how to properly develop people creates a huge competitive edge, which is why only a handful of coaches are successful year after year. Only a handful invest the time to do it.

One particular coach that I admire a lot, perhaps one of the greatest football coaches who ever lived and who's not currently coaching, is Chris Petersen, formerly of Boise State and Washington State. I've never met him, but he only recruited what he called OKGs, "our kind of guys," players he could know, that he could care for, that he could challenge, and that he could reach and teach in the classroom through individual study and hands-on learning. It's why we all stopped to watch the Boise State team play—not because of the blue turf but because we knew they were unique. They did things differently. They weren't the most talented team, yet in 2007, at the Fiesta Bowl, we all remember how Boise State beat the University of Oklahoma.

We only remember it for three reasons: the Statue of Liberty, the hook and ladder, and the marriage proposal at the end of the game. But what won the game was that one coach knew, cared, and then developed and challenged his players. A great coach, Bob Stoops, had not practiced the behaviors they were going to execute when they were successful. After a late OU touchdown, OU had to call a timeout. OU had players in the stands, celebrating an apparent win with fans. They had not rehearsed how they were going to behave after success. I know this because I've spoken to some of the assistant coaches on the Oklahoma side. It's a fascinating game to study. You'll never guess who called the Statue of Liberty play that ended the game: the Boise State backup quarterback, Mike Sanford (also a friend). Mike felt known and trusted enough to make a recommendation. Mike was an OKG.

One challenge that Stran Smith had was that one of his coaches, Dodd Romero, was NOT familiar with rodeo. He was familiar with physical training, mental training, nutrition, health, and recovery. Stran also had a wife who knew him like no other, who could care for him and challenge him like no other. But Stran had a horse to train as well. Stran likes to say that the best thing about rodeo is you don't have a coach, and the worst thing about rodeo is you don't have a coach. He discovered that the one thing he needed to know with absolute certainty was how he learned and developed. Then, he needed to focus his time in that area and eliminate any distractions. Can you imagine the challenge?

Dodd took time to get to know Stran, and then he cared for him. Only then did he challenge Stran. Dodd actually studied rodeo and how ropers rope. He studied the physics of getting off the horse, what was required, etc. Stran was fast when it came to getting off the horse, racing to the calf, and tying a quick knot. Dodd needed to know how it all worked together to develop Stran into a world champion.

Can you imagine how lonely that must have felt? Stran and Dodd had a remarkable connection. Together, they were elite.

Throughout my career, I have been fortunate to have been in the practice pen with many different people. Many were my peers, and some were students of mine. Lots were father-son combinations, and that made me appreciate the way I was coached at a young age.

My first coach was my dad. From the beginning, he knew that I was someone who needed to figure it out on my own. This is so unlike me with my own sons; I have to constantly fight against being a coach with them. I praise and critique every play. My dad was just the opposite. When we were in the practice pen, I might rope all day long, and he'd never say anything. There was no, "Oh, man, that was a great run" or "You know what you messed up there?" He knew that I was a hands-on learner who needed to figure things out on my own. I had to do a lot of figuring, and I needed to go back and watch film, too, but my dad knew this about me when I started roping.

Jennifer and Dodd both fell right in line with this: knowing, caring, and being able to challenge. I might as well throw my mother in there, too, because she didn't know how to rope, but she would coach me probably as much or more than any of them. I would say to her, "You don't even know how to rope," and she would reply, "But I've watched you rope way more than you've ever watched you rope."

I mean, yeah, you're right there.

So, those four were my main coaches. Whether they knew it or not, they all coached me the same way: They let me figure it out. And when the Colonel broke it down for me, I finally understood why I had to make so many extra runs. It was because I was hands-on. I needed that. And then I needed to go back and watch myself on film to figure it out.

The Colonel has hit on something so important here, something that I have watched happen many, many, many times with the father-son, mother-son, father-daughter combinations in the practice pen. To effectively coach these kids, you need to know how they learn. You also need to keep your instruction/coaching positive, and we'll touch on this in a later chapter.

Scan the QR code for bonus video content!

Bonus Video Content!

CHAPTER 9

Can They, Will They, Will Others?

"Assessing and Selecting (hiring) for top talent alone is a recipe for disaster and high turnover rates. The elite ensure they get it right."
–J. Craig Flowers

• • •

BLUF: Once qualified and assessed, the elite ask three questions before hiring. The third question is the most important.

• • •

How do the most elite teams in the world select members for their teams? How do they determine who will be permitted to serve at the top 4% level? Talent is a contributing factor. Each candidate must possess a baseline of skill or talent. Like in any company, a candidate or job applicant must be qualified. Beyond qualifications, however, how do the elite assess, select, and develop members of their organizations? It starts with selecting the right people. They ask three very important questions. I've never heard any company or organization or athletics department ask these questions when considering recruiting someone to their organization. Coach Petersen got close with his OKG method (Our Kind of Guy).

The three questions elite teams ask when they are considering a candidate to join their organization are:

1. **Can they do it?** Is the candidate *truly* qualified, with enough skill?
2. **Will they do it?** Does the candidate have the mental, emotional, physical, and ethical *discipline* required?
3. **Will others do it with them?** Will others be inspired by the candidate, drawn to them, energized by them, and motivated to work alongside them?

Among the elite, if there is ANY hesitation to unequivocally answer "yes" to all of these questions, or any doubt whatsoever, the candidate is not selected. The elite are not willing to allow anyone with any questionable behaviors to infiltrate their organization. The elite will only assess, select, and develop *qualified* candidates who have high character/behavior. They will NOT compromise talent for behavior.

The elite are confident that because of proven processes, as long as someone is qualified AND has high character, they can move from fully qualified to optimal (high talent + high behavior). They have learned that hiring high talent with low character/behavior is a recipe for disaster; introducing toxic behaviors, such as drama, negativity, and questionable commitment to the cause, never works. I'm sure there is an exception. However, I have never seen high talent with low behavior elevate to become OPTIMAL. If you are in the hiring business, hire qualified and fully committed over highly qualified with questionable behavior. Do not risk the cause.

AVOID TOXICITY

Dave Anderson wrote a book entitled *Becoming a Leader of Character*. Prior to becoming an author, Dave led a pharmaceutical sales team. Dave is a friend, and he shared with me how, one night, he tossed and turned, trying to go to sleep. His wife asked him what was wrong. Dave explained that a member of his team was truly talented but also toxic and tearing apart the culture of the organization. His wife said, "You are losing sleep over a toxic employee? Guess who is NOT losing sleep?" Exactly. Dave knew what needed to be done, but he had hesitated because of the team member's talent. The next day, he let the toxic team member go, and team morale soared. "What took you so long?" many wondered.

For too long, leaders tolerate poor behavior because of talent or *perceived* talent. The elite do not. And guess who knows before the leader does? The rest of the team. They are waiting to see if their leader will have the courage and the heart to choose the "harder right" or risk losing full commitment and optimal performance for the sake of talented but toxic employees. Dave told me, "Leaders fail when they hire only for talent. Ultimately, they end up having to fire for behavior."

In NCAA football programs, I've witnessed assistant coaches be incentivized by dollars to recruit five-star talent with zero-star behavior. Once more than 10% of the roster or team consists of players like this, you have no shot of winning consistently. You might win one season. You might even win a Heisman Trophy one year, beat Alabama, or dominate a fiscal year sales cycle. However, in the long term, you have set the conditions for failure.

Some wonder why talent retention is low in their organization. There are two answers to this question. The leader is toxic, or the leader has a tolerance for toxic behavior at the expense of the team.

NFL Quarterback Brock Purdy was "Mr. Irrelevant," meaning he was the last player selected in the NFL draft. He had enough talent to get drafted, and he was FULLY COMMITTED. Purdy has high behavior/character—there is no doubt that he will become OPTIMAL. Patrick Mahomes is a HIGH TALENT, HIGH BEHAVIOR player. Mahomes is OPTIMAL. Both of these players squared off in an unforgettable Super Bowl 2024. They will likely meet again one day soon.

The FULLY COMMITTED will always work to become OPTIMAL (Purdy). Some will never get there (Tommy Halverson), but they still add elite value. However, the highly talented but TOXIC-DRAMA folks love where they are; they love the drama. Can they change? Rarely, if ever. The elite won't take the risk of bringing them on board, and neither should you.

THE FULLY COMMITTED WILL ALWAYS WORK TO BECOME OPTIMAL

Blake Gideon was FULLY COMMITTED. He was a very good player. He never became OPTIMAL, but he was a FULLY COMMITTED TEAMMATE who helped the Broncos win a Super Bowl as a member of the Broncos practice squad.

I was not a great college baseball player. I *was* FULLY COMMITTED. I never became OPTIMAL. Like Stran having to learn a new way to throw his rope, I realized the only way I was going to be able to play college baseball was to add unique value. I needed to become *uniquely qualified* and FULLY COMMITTED to have a chance.

At the age of 15, I read a *Reader's Digest* article about the late Pete Rose (well before the gambling issues became a part of his life). In the article, "Charlie Hustle" said that the only way he was able to play beyond high school was to become a switch hitter. I carefully tore out the article and taped it to my bedroom mirror.

We lived in the original hospital at West Point, built in 1852, which had been turned into a set of officers' quarters (Dad was a lieutenant colonel). My bedroom was the main surgery room of the hospital. It was sorta creepy, frankly. It was a big room, large enough for me to swing a baseball bat. Immediately after taping that article to the mirror, I uncapped my green 33/29 aluminum Easton baseball bat, filled it with rocks from underneath the patio porch, and taped it shut. Then I made a promise to myself to only swing the bat left-handed for the next 60 days.

Each day, I would carry an old bag of baseballs my dad had gathered down to the Hudson River, where there was a chain-link fence. There, I would hit baseballs off of a tee, left-handed, for hours. The first ball I hit off the tee actually went into the Hudson River. I didn't even hit the fence five feet in front of me. I thought, *I'm going to run out of baseballs.*

Nearly every day for two months, I had to say "no thank you" to those who invited me to go swimming, eat pizza, go fishing, or do some other extracurricular activity. For 60 days, I did not swing the bat right-handed. Before I went to bed every night, I swung the bat left-handed five hundred times. Dad would walk in sometimes late at night and just smile.

Sometime around the 45th day, a teammate called to ask me to do something; I can't remember what. "I've got to go hit," I told him, and he said, "I'll go with you." His name is Craig Cairns, and today, he *owns* a wealth management company in Rochester, NY: Howe and Rusling Inc. Craig flew Apache helicopters in Desert Storm and was our high school catcher. He was a great, all-around athlete and an OPTIMAL friend who helped me become a switch hitter.

The first time I stepped into the left-hander batter's box during a game, I could hear someone in the dugout say, "What is he doing?" I remember exactly who it was (Jose). The dugout went silent. My heart was racing. I took the first pitch. With the next pitch, I started winding up at the plate as the pitcher wound up on the mound. Somehow, I hit a line drive down the left field line. I swung late (which I continued to do at TCU) and ended up standing on second base with a double.

I remember this moment like it was last week. I looked over at the dugout, and everybody was cheering. I stood there, looking at the dugout, thinking, "Where were you guys the last 60 days?" My best friend to this day, Craig Cairns, was in the bullpen, warming up a pitcher. I looked out at him, and he took his hat off and tipped it to me. The only guy in my high school class who was invited to my wedding was the guy who went down to the Hudson River with me and helped me become a switch hitter, allowing me to play at Texas Christian University (TCU).

We didn't win a championship. However, at TCU, I made lifelong friends and business partners, all because I FULLY COMMITTED to becoming a switch hitter. Decisions like that are often made when no one's around, when no one's cheering, when people think you're crazy. Those can be the most valuable decisions a person will ever make. Writing this book for example, there were those who doubted we would do it.

I threw out the ceremonial first pitch a couple of years ago at the Army West Point vs TCU baseball game in Fort Worth (I didn't bounce it; it *was* a *little* high and outside). Teammates, family, and our assistant coach from 1984, Dave Smotzer, attended. About two hundred folks, including spouses, went to Joe T. Garcia's for dinner afterward. Our TCU Coach, Dave Schmotzer came up to me and said, "You know what this is all about?"

"No," I said. "Honestly, I can't believe it. I was not a great player."

"Smotz" put his arm around me and said, "This is about being a great teammate."

Be FULLY COMMITTED. Hire FULLY COMMITTED. Cut the talented yet toxic folks from your life and organization. The second- and third-order effects will last a lifetime. When Stran Smith started the process to become a world champion, he was fully committed. He was not optimal, but he believed that if he remained fully committed, situationally, and self-aware and then took the necessary action, one day, he would have the chance, not the guarantee, to become optimal. Spend your time with the fully committed and the optimal, not with those who doubt you, who bring toxic energy and negativity into your lives. You don't need the drama. The most elite in the world have no room for drama and negativity.

Scan the QR code for bonus video content!

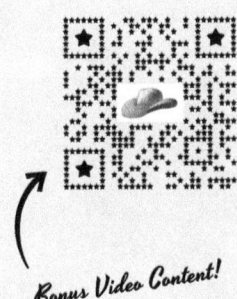

Bonus Video Content!

CHAPTER 10

Service and Leadership

"I came by your office, you weren't here. I'm glad you weren't. The more time you are out of the office spending time with the personnel you're charged to serve, the better we will become."
–a note left on my desk at West Point by General Mike Scaparrotti, aka "Scap," August 2005

• • •

BLUF: Less email and more face-to-face communication are great choices.

• • •

In July 2002, after serving four years overseas in France and North Africa, I had the opportunity to request my next assignment, and I requested West Point. After teaching in the foreign language department under Colonel Woody Held (a great leader) from 2002 to 2005, I was named Director of Cadet Activities (DCA). A somewhat similar position at a civilian university would be the vice chancellor of student affairs.

My predecessor did a remarkable job of preparing me for one of the most challenging positions at West Point. We had a 90-day overlap, and he wore me out with candid and critical information. Lieutenant Colonel Tom Endres, a pilot, had served alongside some of the same elite units I had supported.

He specifically mentioned how hard a group of ladies had worked in one of our ten restaurant operations, Grant Hall.

Note: *West Point encompasses 16,000 acres and is our nation's longest continuously occupied military reservation. In my opinion, every American should visit Normandy, France, Arlington Cemetery, or West Point.*

I thought about our time in France. I was the American exchange officer at the French Staff College. In our class was a British Royal Marine, Nicholas Nottingham (a proper British name). One particular afternoon, I was running late to get to a meeting. As I imagine most British Royal Marines are when they are not serving in combat, Nick Nottingham was leaning against the wall with one hand elegantly inside his military coat. When I ran by him, out of breath, he stopped me and, with a *very* British accent, said, "JC, never run in front of the soldiers. It makes them nervous."

I wanted to lead well. However, I had to be disciplined. I needed to "not run in front of our organization." Furniture didn't need to be hastily and mindlessly rearranged to make it look like I was having an impact. Instead, I needed to remain calm, focused, and curious.

For 90 days, I met with no more than four civilian employees a day. I asked each person to share one thing we did really well and should keep doing. I also asked for one thing we needed to improve on or start doing that we currently were not. I needed to know them. Then, I needed to care for them, and eventually, I would be able to challenge them.

After 90 days, I felt I had enough information to make a decision. I determined with the help of a dear friend, Lieutenant Colonel Jim Whaley, an Army helicopter pilot, that all of our behaviors in our organization could be driven by one simple phrase, similar to what you read earlier in this book when Ben Hunt Davis spent a year asking himself, "Will it make the boat go faster?" Our one phrase, which has since withstood 20 years of possible change, was "All for the Corps." Everything we thought about, did, or considered would be driven by one question: is it "All for the Corps?"

If the answer was yes, my directive, my guidance, was "execute" (do it). I told the entire organization at our first all-hands meeting that responsibility for our cash position (our profits and losses) was mine alone. Their *only* focus was to execute duties with an "All for the Corps" mindset: create, innovate, execute.

The Directorate of Cadet Activities is a non-appropriated funded entity, meaning Congress does not appropriate government funds for it. We had to earn money and make a payroll. There was one active-duty military member; everyone else was a civilian (several hundred people). We were a for-profit organization. We had two retail stores with thousands of SKUs working on 16–22% margins. We turned over annual inventories five times (that's a crazy churn).

Along with Eisenhower Hall Theatre (IkeHall.com), we had about ten restaurant operations, from sit-down dining to coffee shops, scattered throughout campus. All of these business centers needed to earn dollars to support our nation's most co-curricular activities program, contributing to the development of West Point cadets so they graduated as leaders of character committed to duty, honor, and country. We became extremely profitable in 24 months. Why? The entire organization innovated, created, and operated with a new mindset, an "All for the Corps" mindset.

"All for the Corps" became the one thing everyone could do and be. Frankly, it became easy for us to operate. Morale soared, and we began to attract the most talented people at West Point to work with us. For the next six years, I had a hard time sleeping because I couldn't wait to get into the office each morning. I recalled Colonel Magruder (who would later rise to the rank of three star general) sitting in his office, writing notes to soldiers back in 1988. I remembered the Pentagon's message from when we'd been living in Morocco, the one with the two soldiers meeting at a bar and then, later the next morning, running at the track: "I don't know, but he's out here every day." We were applying the same principles I had learned and witnessed while serving the most elite teams on the planet. These same behaviors and mindsets worked to perfection in all of our business enterprises. It worked, and it can work for you as well.

Remember the ladies at Grant Hall that my predecessor mentioned during our overlap? They needed to be known, cared for, and then, perhaps, challenged. I met weekly with our director of restaurants, and he informed me that the ladies in Grant Hall had sold 242,000 sandwiches over a 12-month period (imagine a five-star Subway restaurant in a Harry Potter-type setting—that is Grant Hall).

I asked Kevin, the food and beverage manager, to schedule a meeting when the restaurant was not busy so I could talk with them and understand exactly what it took to make 242,000 sandwiches. On the day of the meeting, I arrived at Grant Hall and immediately went behind the counter. I introduced myself with my first and last name. I wore a military uniform, and they could see my rank. I learned from the elite to never lead with rank. In *that* world, for many reasons, it's almost always first names, call signs, or nicknames. It's about the cause, not one's rank.

I got to know each of the eight to ten ladies behind the counter and asked them to show me how to make a sandwich. Then I put on an apron and began to construct what I thought was a pretty good "sammy." It turned out to be a dilapidated pile of meat, bread, and vegetables and a mélange of three sauces (I purposefully asked them to show me how to make the most difficult sandwich). It was a sloppy mess, but this wasn't about my sandwich. We had a good laugh as I tried to replicate what they had done over 240,000 times. This meeting lasted 90 minutes. I did not rush. I never looked at my watch. I never looked at my phone. I focused on them.

When I asked them what the most difficult part of their job was, they immediately looked at their supervisors. Kevin and Maria nodded as if to say, "Go ahead, speak freely." The women explained that every time they handed a sandwich to the customer across the glass counter, the counter struck them in their chests. At the end of the day, their chests were sore. I touched the counter and watched them demonstrate exactly how the poorly placed counter impacted them physically. Kevin said, "We can easily fix that. I'm going to call right now and have a contractor come over tomorrow to change it." The women were elated. I asked them what their feet felt like at the end of the day, and after they explained how sore their feet would get, I asked Kevin to install professional kitchen padding for foot comfort.

Another easy win. Later, I took it a step further. We had a relationship with the West Point athletics department, and after doing some horse trading, we got them some comfortable shoes, the same ones issued to many of the athletes.

Once the meeting was over, I thanked the women, handed out some awards, and left Grant Hall. That 90-minute visit turned out to be one of the most important things I ever did in the restaurant business. Getting to know those ladies, feeling what they went through, and caring for them while acknowledging their accomplishment of making over 200,000 sandwiches was important (it was *not* difficult). When I asked them what our mission was, they smiled and said, "All for the Corps, sir."

Judges 3:31 and 5:5–6 are about a simple farmer, Shamgar, an Israelite. Shamgar lived in the days when the Philistines were running rampant in Israel, and there was no king. He got fed up with the gang of thieving Philistines running around, making travel impossible on the roadways. You had to take back roads when you were going somewhere because you would get robbed and mugged. There was no law. Shamgar, a simple farmer, took it upon himself to use what he had, which was an ox goad. The goad, a long stick between five and seven feet long, was used to drive oxen while you were plowing. One end was blunt, and one end was sharp. Shamgar killed six

hundred Philistine warriors who were raiding and robbing people, all with just an ox goad.

Why?

He used what he had, right where he was. To me, that is the ultimate service to a cause. There are many stories like this in the Bible. In the story of David, one of my favorites, he used a rock and a sling to take down a Philistine giant, Goliath. And by the way, the Bible tells us that David had five stones. The reason for that was that Goliath had four brothers. David, however, didn't have to deal with the other four after he took care of Goliath.

No matter who you are or where you are in your life, you can be of service to a cause. God will use you right where you are. He's equipped you with the tools to do whatever He's called you to do. Whether it's a rope, an ox goad, your influence, or your voice, God has put you in the right position to use it. Maybe it's one of the tools you've learned about in this book. For me, it was the process of learning and putting the right people in my life to help me become the husband, father, friend, and son that God has called me to be at this stage in my life. This has been the ultimate service to a cause. He has brought these people into my life at just the right time.

Nowadays, it's easy to get overwhelmed. I've got 18 different things going at once, and I'm trying to keep all these plates spinning. One day, I was driving down the road, probably driving too fast, running late, and the phone rang. It was Pastor Matthew Hagee. We started chatting, and he asked me how I was doing. I started venting to him just a little about all the craziness of my life. Then he said something that resonated with me so much that I had to pull over to write it down. He said, "You're busy because you have a purpose. And if you didn't have a purpose, then you would be bored. I would rather be busy on purpose than bored and worthless."

At that time in my life, I feel like God was asking me, *"What's the difference between a job and your purpose?"* So, I looked up the definition of a "job." It's defined as a paid position of regular employment, a specific task, or a piece of work for a period. "Purpose" is the reason for which something was made.

I got to thinking: *Am I a dad because it's my job? Am I a husband because it's my job? Am I a friend because it's my job?*

The answer was clear: "No. Being a dad, husband, and friend are the roles for which I was made."

One of the biggest mistakes we make is to focus only on ourselves. We will touch on this in the next chapter, but it's got a lot to do with your ego and me, mine, and I.

Really, though, my purpose is to have balance in my life. To do that, I must put God first and surround myself with like-minded people. For me, the ultimate service to a cause is being used by Him for His purpose.

Leadership is service to a cause: faith, family, friends, community, teams, and self. Stran was relentless on his path to winning a gold buckle. He worked very hard. No one was going to outwork him. But at the age of 26, all the way to the age of 32, was Stran Smith, my close friend, selfless? I think if you had asked him that back then, he would have said, yes, spiritually, he was. He was exactly where he needed to be, but it wasn't until Dodd Romero came into his life that his purpose became aligned with a process that he could.

Dodd gave him a real process he could trust. What do I mean by that? Well, up until that moment, Stran just thought he was going to outwork everybody on a path to becoming a world champion. It hadn't happened. For whatever reason, it wasn't God's timing yet. But at 38, Stran's process of outworking everyone and sacrificing his body with every run was no longer going to work. Without a real process and Dodd Romero in his life, the incredible journey would have ended without a gold buckle.

When in doubt, Stran would turn the lights on and rope until two, three, and four in the morning. It wasn't until Dodd came into his life and said,

"Doing that is actually not selfless; it's SELFISH. Your body has to recover, Stran. Clean nutrition, great hydration, great rest and recovery, strength training, and cardio are all part of the process. If you want to have a real opportunity, a real path to winning the gold buckle, you'd better trust this process." No one could have told a 20-something-year-old Stran Smith that. His amygdala was hijacked.

An authentic, relentless, and selfless friend who ended up being a coach, Dodd Romero, entered Stran's life at exactly the right time and put in place everything that Stran needed to get on a path to becoming a world champion at the age of 38, something that may not be repeated ever again in the history of rodeo—like Nolan Ryan's seven no-hitters or Cal Ripken's streak.

I work with CEOs, presidents, elite athletes, and coaches making millions a year. When I apply the crawl, walk, run approach and sit down to get to know them, I'll casually ask, "What is the mission of the organization that you've been asked to lead?" Most of the time, they're able to tell me the mission. Simon Sinek often says, "We're not going to get into a discussion about mission and vision because those are two different things." So, let's skip over *vision* for a moment. Let's get to values. Values are behaviors. When I ask these name leaders, CEOs, head coaches, and presidents what their missions and values are, I often discover blind spots.

Yes, they're written on beautifully framed posters throughout the office, and in some cases, they're put on large signs so that every student-athlete who comes for a visit to the university can look up and see words like "family," "integrity," "commitment," and "discipline." But it doesn't take long to realize that many—not all, but many—named leaders in positions of authority are not able to articulate clearly the mission and values of the organization or team they're charged with leading.

Faith, family, friends, community, teams, and self—each of those has a mission and an associated set of behaviors, also known as values. Yes, even a family can have a mission and value statement. It sounds quite "cray cray," but my wife and I have sat down with our daughters and talked about the mission of our family and the behaviors associated with it, and slowly but surely, this leads to discussions on the other six causes.

The same principles I was exposed to for a decade, when applied to a business model, worked to perfection. Real processes—*Know, Care,* and *Challenge*; authentic, relentless, and selfless service—are always the right things to do.

Scan the QR code for bonus video content!

Bonus Video Content!

CHAPTER 11

Ego Is a Distraction: A Sense of Humor Is a Competitive Edge

"Some of the most elite leaders I've ever known had a great sense of humor. They were the first to laugh at themselves. Most of the poorest leaders I've known were exactly the opposite."
–J. Craig Flowers

BLUF: Be the first to laugh at yourself, the last to take credit, and *the* one who accepts responsibility.

In 1990, I was a newly promoted Army captain with orders to Fort Chaffee, Arkansas. In four weeks, I was directed to report to my new assignment. I had done well. However, I was not among the top five in our class of 60 captains. I had classmates who were more tactically skilled and much smarter.

However, in the back of the classroom, wearing khaki cargo pants and a white polo shirt (with a popped collar), a fit gentleman with long hair and a gray beard said he wanted to meet with me in a private room. My orders to the Joint Readiness Training Center had been amended. I was diverted to the East Coast.

Six months into the new assignment, still not knowing what had occurred, I asked him why I was chosen. The answer stunned me, but it also reassured me that the system used to identify unique attributes for unique assignments was accurate: "We needed someone who had performed well (top 10%) in a conventional military assignment. After we narrowed the field, we looked for three attributes in evaluation reports for year group 1986: *innovative thinking, creativity, and a sense of humor*."

There aren't many officers in the army inventory who consistently use those three things in their report cards. I chuckled. *Their process* had worked. I would not have done well in the conventional Army. At some point, I needed to innovate, create, and operate.

Large, conventional organizations have lots of rules and regulations, making it difficult for personnel to innovate and create. When you get out of line, start to innovate, and create, you are viewed as going rogue, being noncompliant, or not being "a company man." I wore the fact that *they* had identified a *sense of humor* in my officer efficiency reports as a badge of honor. I laughed at myself first when I made mistakes. The mistakes I made weren't life-or-death ones. Heck, most of the time, when senior officers or peers laughed at my mistakes, I laughed with them. Mine were silly mistakes.

During a training event, I put plastic bags on my feet before a 12-mile road march with hardened light infantrymen, mostly Rangers (which I am not). Yep, I did that. It was raining, and I didn't want my feet to get wet. For the first two miles, my feet were dry! The next 10 miles told a different story. I was 22. I didn't know much about the Army and didn't speak their language. I didn't know the rhythms or their routines. I often made mistakes that someone who had been a Boy Scout, Cub Scout, or Eagle Scout probably would not have made.

In college, I played baseball and wasn't committed to learning military "stuff." I believe the only reason I was selected to go into *the program* was because of the locker room. In the locker room, one must have thick skin. You have to be the first to embrace it when you're the punchline of a joke. Baseball is a game of failure, thick skin, and short memory. The ability to laugh at oneself is important for success in baseball and life.

TAMING THE EGO

Flash ahead to West Point, sometime around 2007. I was asked to escort about 40 cadets from the banks of the mighty Hudson River to New York City, 58 miles south, so that we would board Steve Forbes's yacht, *Highlander*. Look it up. It's one helluva vessel.

I was looking forward to taking the three-hour boat ride aboard the *Highlander* all the way back up to West Point, where Steve Forbes, his wife, some family members, and about a hundred successful businessmen and women and their spouses would take in an Army football game at Michie Stadium. Miss Beth was with me, and as we were standing in the receiving line before boarding the yacht, she asked me what I was going to say to Mr. Forbes.

I smiled rather confidently at her and said, "You won't believe what I'm about to do."

"Please don't embarrass me," she replied.

As all the CEOs and presidents made their way through the receiving line, they all fawned over Mr. Forbes, telling him what an honor and a pleasure it was to meet him (etc., etc.). Then I found myself in front of him and his lovely wife. I shook his hand, thanked him for hosting the 40 cadets, along with my wife and me, and then said, "We would love to hear what it was like when you hosted *Saturday Night Live*."

Mr. Forbes lit up. His face became animated, and he said to the assistant standing in the receiving line, "Make sure that I get to spend time with them."

We boarded the *Highlander* and were underway sometime around 8 a.m. Within minutes of us leaving the harbor, Mr. Forbes came and found me and my wife. For 45 minutes, he sat with us and told us in detail what it was like to host *Saturday Night Live*. It was fascinating. The conversation was very comfortable. It went back and forth, and after about 45 minutes, I realized that there were plenty of business leaders hovering around our table, wanting to get just five minutes with Mr. Forbes. However, because of the question I had asked in the receiving line, he had spent nearly an hour seated with just Miss Beth and me.

Finally, I said, "Mr. Forbes, you've been very generous with your time. There are a lot of people who want to spend time with you on this three-hour journey, and I want to give them the courtesy that they deserve."

"Oh, I know," he replied, "but this was something that no one ever asked me, and I'm so glad I got to tell that story." Then he got up and started mingling with the other people aboard the *Highlander*.

At that point, I took a deep breath, smiled rather arrogantly to Miss Beth, and said something I've heard Stran Smith say on occasion: "What do you think of them apples?"

Miss Beth smiled at me gently and said, "Honey, where are the cadets?"

The 40 cadets that I was charged with leading aboard the *Highlander* were nowhere to be found. I immediately realized that I had forgotten my mission. I raced to the top floor of the *Highlander*. No cadets. They would have been easy to spot because they were wearing white tops over white pants.

I went to the second and third floors: no cadets. Finally, I walked down to the lowest level of the ship. There was a large ice sculpture of a swan, four feet tall, standing in the center of a beautiful wooden table. Around that swan was the most beautiful display of giant boiled shrimp I had ever seen.

And around that shrimp were 40 cadets dressed in white over white, consuming as much of it as fast as they could. They were grunting with joy. They had cocktail sauce on their white uniforms. There were shrimp tails and shells everywhere. They couldn't even talk. Some were not even aware I was there. They were in a shrimp coma. Miss Beth came down the stairs and immediately grabbed a few slices of lemon to get the cocktail sauce stains off their white uniforms.

I was so caught up in asking the exact right question so my wife and I could spend time with Mr. Forbes that I had forgotten what my mission was. My ego was the distraction.

I gathered the cadets up, smiled, and said, "Ladies and gentlemen, I have let you down. I got so caught up in spending time with Mr. Forbes that I failed to inform you of what your mission is aboard this ship. We are to spend time with these business leaders, with these leaders of the industry. We are to mix and mingle with this crowd of over a hundred to share the West Point story and welcome them to the birthplace of leadership, your alma mater, which we will arrive at in 90 minutes." I'd gotten so caught up in my own agenda that I'd forgotten what my true north was.

I think of that story often. I became distracted NOT by a smartphone but by Steve Forbes and the drama of being aboard his yacht. My ego got in the way of my mission. It's funny now. Actually, it was funny then, too.

The great Nolan Ryan shared a story at our TCU alumni baseball banquet a few years ago. I will try to do the story justice. It is a great example of how ego can get in the way of reality. I love Nolan Ryan and his family. His favorite catcher was a native Texan and NY Met—the late Jerry Grote. Jerry and my father were close friends growing up in San Antonio, Texas.

The morning after Nolan had thrown his seventh no-hitter (a record that will probably never be broken), he was seated in a Denny's restaurant, ordering breakfast. The entire back page of *USA Today* had a picture of him, along with an article describing not only the seventh no-hitter but the six previous.

The waiter approached the table and took Nolan's order. Nolan could tell that the waiter recognized him because, as the young man was returning to the kitchen, he stopped to talk to a couple of the other employees, probably to tell them, "That's Nolan Ryan." When the waiter returned with a cup of coffee and a glass of orange juice, and with the *USA Today* newspaper lying in front of Nolan on the table, he said, "Why, you are Nolan Ryan, aren't you?"

"Yeah, I am," Nolan replied.

Then the waiter said something that Nolan Ryan appreciated very much. Despite being the subject of the entire back page of the newspaper lying there on the table, the waiter asked, "Well, whatcha doin' these days? Coaching?"

After telling the story, Nolan said, "So, just about the time you think that everyone is paying attention to your accomplishments, someone will come along and remind you that most of the world is not." It's up to you to stay focused, knowing that ego is your enemy and humor is how some of the most elite teams on the planet deal with stress and strain.

I think that learning to laugh at yourself is one of the key components to keeping your ego in check. I rodeoed for 20 years professionally, and as the Colonel said in his story about playing baseball at TCU, you need to have thick skin, and you can't be afraid to laugh at yourself. Rodeo professionals travel nearly 11 months out of the year, and there's a lot of travel and downtime in between performances. Cowboys end up spending a lot of time with other alpha males. We're all extremely competitive, but there is a camaraderie there as well. It leads to a lot of razzing and practical jokes, which, I think, is healthy.

That's one of the things I think is wrong with society today. We're so busy getting offended or being afraid we're going to offend somebody that we forget to have a sense of humor. So, I think that it's very important that you learn how to laugh at yourself and have fun in high-pressure situations.

John 10:10 says, *"I came that they may have life and have it abundantly."* I think one meaning of an abundant life is enjoying it and having fun. Enjoy the struggle and enjoy the wins. That's my advice for myself and my family.

A lot of my family members have competed at high levels. Several of my nephews rodeoed and even won their own World Championships. As for my boys, one plays college baseball, and my oldest throws the discus and hammer at the college level. My last-minute advice to them, every time, is, "Hey, go have fun." It's that simple. You know what to do, so be yourself and have fun.

My dad was a great person when it came to laughing at himself, and he was probably the humblest human I have ever met. See, my dad was the first person to make the National Finals Rodeo and dismount on the right side of the horse. Everybody used to get off on the left, but he started dismounting on the right.

The reason to get off on the right is that it is faster. In calf roping, you always throw the calf down from the right side, but traditionally, cowboys always got on and off on the left. It took more time to dismount the traditional way, duck under your rope, and run to the calf. Traditional cowboy wisdom said that if you got off on the right side, it would ruin your horse by making it duck away from you and the rope. From the time rodeo began in the late 1800s up until 1960, that's how calf roping at the National Finals was always done—you got off on the left as cowboys had done for centuries.

Now, let me tell you a little about my dad, Clifton Smith. I was the last of five kids. Dad worked two jobs: running the ranch and working for the railroad. He rodeoed on the side, but he would still make the National Finals rodeo. His nickname back in the day was Snake or Rattler because they said he was poisonous. The most rodeos he ever went to in a year was 38, while other guys would go to as many as 100 to make the finals. If he went to three or four rodeos, he either won or placed at nearly all of them. He was probably one of the greatest ropers of his time, but he never really got the recognition because he didn't rodeo full time. He had a family at home, and he wasn't willing to neglect his responsibilities to them. My dad is the perfect example of what we talked about in Chapter 10: faith, family, friends, community, teams, and self.

Years later, Dad was at the NFR as a spectator. By this time, he had a son and four grandsons competing, with three world champions among them. He was being interviewed about the right-side dismount, and the interviewer said, "You know, you kind of started all this, and you changed how the sport is done. What possessed you to start getting off on the right? If it was supposed to ruin your horse, why would you do that?"

At that moment, my dad could have reflected on all the success our family has had, thumped his chest, and said, "Yes, I really did change the sport! This was all because of me!" Instead, in his typical, matter-of-fact fashion, he simply said in his dry, West Texas drawl, "Well, the reason I got off on the right was because it was faster. The interviewer replied, "I thought that would ruin your horse?" To which my dad replied, "Aww, my horse wasn't much a count anyhow."

To the non-Texans, what he meant was Dad didn't think his horse was worth a lot of money anyway because he didn't pay a bunch of money for him, having raised him from birth. Don't get it wrong, that horse was WORTH a whole lot, he just didn't COST a whole lot. And my dad knew that getting off on the right wasn't going to ruin him either, but he's too humble to say so. That is my dad to a T. He was the epitome of not having an ego, not taking things too seriously, and not tooting your own horn.

I've successfully jumped out of an airplane with a parachute eight times. To someone who has never jumped out of an airplane with a parachute, that may seem like a lot, but to those I served alongside, it's hardly a blip. All eight jumps I made in the military were what are called "Hollywood" jumps. They were not in combat. Some were with combat equipment and at night (training). The last jump that I made was in France with the French parachute division.

When they issued me the parachute, which was much smaller than the American parachutes I was used to, they laughed and said, "It may not be as big as the American canopy, but it's better quality. Besides, if it does not work, bring it back, and we'll gladly replace it" (read that again with a Pepé Le Pew accent).

We trained that afternoon, familiarizing ourselves with new equipment and going through the scenarios of what would happen if the parachute malfunctioned. Due to my poor exit on the third jump that day, I had a malfunction. It was my fault. All the risers were twisted above my head, forcing my chin into my chest. The canopy was about 30% deployed, and I was descending faster than the others—a lot faster. As I was going through the process of addressing the issue, I recalled how one of the trainers, earlier in the day, had said, "If you have a malfunction, remember, you have plenty of time. In fact, you have the rest of your life" (again with that Pepé accent). I was actually smiling to myself as I worked to fix the issue.

My time was limited. I was situational aware and self-aware, and we had trained the process to deal with this exact situation. If I stuck to the process, I was certain of a positive outcome. Even during the darkest times, some of the most elite in the world will use humor as a way to keep things loose and reduce anxiety and stress. They know, because of the trust that they develop with their teammates, that it's never personal. I went through the process of untangling my parachute risers. The canopy fully deployed at about eight hundred feet, and I landed just fine.

I was a less-than-average college baseball player. I started a handful of mid-week games and went through a two-year hitting slump, lol. One of my teammates wrote on the bathroom stall, "Flowers should bat without a bat." All that did was motivate me and make me laugh when I read it. There was some truth to it, but they were also trying to loosen me up and get me out of the slump.

Finally, I'm reminded of a joke:

A patient meets with a doctor after tests are run. The doctor says, "I've got some good news and bad news."

Patient: "Give me the good news, doc."

Doc: "The good news is you've got 24 hours to live."

Patient: "My gosh! What could be the BAD news?"

Doc: "I couldn't get in touch with you yesterday."

Scan the QR code for bonus video content!

Bonus Video Content!

CHAPTER 12

What Field Are You Playing In?

"Be where you are supposed to be, doing what you are supposed to be doing, with the people you are supposed to be doing it with, at THE TIME you are supposed to be doing it. If you do that, trouble will have a hard time finding you."
–Coach Alan Wartes, Air It Out Football Camp

• • •

BLUF: Motivation is a by-product of an action. Waiting to 'become motivated' is weakness. Execute.

• • •

We all spend time in an arena. For me, it was literally a rodeo arena. Now, yours might not be a rodeo arena. It might be a baseball diamond or a football field. It could be an auditorium. Some of these arenas are filled with hundreds, if not thousands, of sets of eyes. For others, your arena could be a classroom, a boardroom, or even a breakfast table with one or two sets of sleepy little eyes looking at you. We are walking into some type of arena, no matter what we do in life.

We have a choice. Is this going to be a positive arena, or is it going to be a negative one? We get to decide if the arena will be a leadership laboratory or a self-centered box. We choose. Deuteronomy 30:19 says, *"This day I set before you life and death, blessings and curses."* "Choose life. Choose me," God ultimately says. It's our choice. My question to you is, how do you lead? More importantly, how do you lead yourself? Before you can lead others, you must lead yourself.

I put together a list of one-word descriptions that will help you identify what arena you are in and I will share it at the end of this chapter. The list came from Galatians 5, which tells us of the fruits of the Spirit; Matthew 5, where Jesus presents us with the Beatitudes; and 1 Corinthians 13, which tells us about what love is and is not. I use this list to identify if I am in a positive or negative arena. Am I acting out of love, joy, peace, patience, kindness, and self-control, or am I using hate, fear, doubt, and unbelief? Am I worrying? You can use this list to give yourself a check. If you're a fearful person, you're probably going to use fear as your go-to. You will lead out of fear.

If you don't give yourself much grace, you're probably not going to be a leader who gives very much grace. But if you lead out of love, if you lead out of kindness, if you have patience, you're probably going to be a kind and patient leader, the kind of leader others want to follow. I use three simple questions to make sure I know where I'm leading from:

1. Where will I start?
2. How will I walk it out?
3. How will I finish?

Let's start with the easiest one of the three: how you start. Matthew 6:33 says, *"Seek ye first the kingdom of God, and all you need will be given to you."* Before you walk into the arena, you have to get your mind right. How do you get your mind right? Use the words from the list. Am I happy? Do I have peace? Am I walking in love? Or am I nervous? Am I anxious? Am I doubting myself or others? Am I allowing fear to overcome me?

This is a good checklist to see if you're starting off in the right arena and not getting off track in the wrong one. If you start off in the wrong arena, it's almost impossible to end up in the right one, so this is extremely important.

Start off positive, full of love, full of joy, full of peace. That's why this all starts with you first. You have to lead yourself and choose to ride into your arena with the right mindset before you can lead others.

Next is how you walk it out. When you encounter a challenge, what is your first response? On your way to work, when somebody cuts you off in traffic and gives you the one-finger wave, what's your first response? How do you walk it out? You see, the elite don't jump over to the negatives when faced with a challenge. They start in the right arena, but when things come up, practicing discipline kicks in, and having real processes in place keeps you in the right arena. You have to stay in the positive arena. Stay humble and full of joy. Don't let a situation cause you to switch to the other arena into doubt, fear, anger, and unbelief.

The last thing is, how do you finish? Many men and women have started strong and finished badly. You know, when I think of how you finish, I think of *SportsCenter*.

ESPN has built an entire network around "the finish." We celebrate athletes because of their ability to be their best at the most critical time of the game (the end). Why do we celebrate athletes? Because they do uncommon things. They're the elite, especially the ones who make the *SportsCenter* "Top 10 Moments." Think about all the blood, sweat, and tears that have been poured into an athlete, an individual, to be able to come through in the middle of the second quarter or a touchdown run at the beginning of the third quarter. It's always the last-second shot. It's the walk-off home run. It's the tenth go-round win. That's what we celebrate. Why? Because it's the finish. Everybody dreams of hitting the last-second shot.

We want to finish strong.

We want to be able to set ourselves up for success, which comes down to how you lead, how you walk it out, how you perform, and how you finish. What determines if you win the right way or not? Whatever you do regularly will determine what you eventually have. That's what we hope to teach you with this book.

Earlier, we talked about instructive organizations versus constructive organizations. Applying the 80% constructive to 20% instructive not only works in organizations but also with self-talk.

The words that we think about, the words that Stran has included in this book that he uses to ensure that he's properly aligned and in the right arena, lead to constructive development. One of the six causes that we talk about often is self. When Stran mentions that serving or leading oneself is the first step to serving in those other causes, he's exactly right. Positive words ensure that you're aligned with serving the self, not because you're selfish but because you're selfless. By using them, you will find it rather easy and natural to serve in your faith, family, friend group, and community and on the teams that you have the opportunity to lead, whether that's in the office, a volunteer program, athletics, or education.

Service to a cause—that's leadership.

When one of your close friends and business partners is Stran Smith, you get to spend time in Childress, Texas, and each hour there is an adventure. One morning, you're sitting in Dawson's Cafe, eating Stran's favorite lunch order (Dawson's keeps special "Stran Bread" on hand, btw—ask for it). The next hour, you may find yourself out at the STS Ranch, and then a couple of hours later, you're in the 1930 Remnant store just off HWY 287, talking about STS Ranchwear ladies' handbags.

On a recent trip to Childress, Stran had another cowboy chore he needed to knock out—a routine task for him but something I wasn't familiar with. He said, "Hop in the truck. We've got to go over and load a bull." I was wearing khaki pants, the wrong shoes, and a Polo shirt. Stran, well, he's always dressed like a cowboy in jeans, a long-sleeve shirt, boots, belt, and a cowboy hat.

As we pulled out of the gate on HWY 287, took a right, and headed over to the bull pasture, I could see that the customer had already backed up his trailer and was anxious to load the bull that he had agreed to purchase from Stran. We were in a hurry.

The moment we stopped next to the pen housing three bulls, I watched Stran Smith transform himself from a rushed, caffeinated, high-energy businessman full of ideas, to a gentle, focused, situationally and self-aware leader. He had a process. He mumbled something under his breath as he got out of the truck, and I watched his body language change as he opened the gate. What I remember him saying was, "I got to keep an eye out on that one." Then, with a stick about six feet long, he positioned himself in the pen and gently communicated through a series of arm and hand signals and odd cowboy sounds that he was in charge.

The targeted beast was inspired to easily be loaded onto the trailer. The customer was so excited to own this bull. Stran left the pen, shut the gate, and locked the bull inside the trailer. Then he gave me a cowboy grin and said, "They're not always that easy." Without knowing, I had complicated the process by getting out of the truck. I had become a distraction for some of the bulls and people involved, but I'm sure glad I did get out because I got to witness what most will never have the chance to see: a man comfortable in his arena and applying all the principles of gentle service to a cause. At that moment, I saw Stran in an arena where he was extremely comfortable operating.

What's interesting about that is we can all apply those same principles in our own lives. The elite recognize the situation they're in. Whether it's filled with stress or with peace, they are able to fluently align themselves with the situation and use it as a developmental experience while at the same time accomplishing what they need to do.

After the bull was successfully and safely loaded, Stran got in the truck, and we had a good laugh. As we drove through Childress, I started thinking, "What if Stran had jumped out of the truck, leaped over the fence, and started yelling, cursing, and demonstrating that he was in a hurry, that he was late, that he was panicked. How would those bulls have behaved in that scenario?"

Well, we've seen exactly how members of teams behave when the leader panics, when the leader is frustrated, when the leader is not in control, and when the leader is afraid and *only* instructive. The bull *might* have loaded, but you can bet that it would have been panicked and anxious—and it would probably have been the last bull that was sold to that customer. So many times, coaches, leaders, senior military officials, and politicians think that leading with fear and anxiety is a way to get things done. Over time, it doesn't work.

Remember Nicholas Nottingham, the British Royal Marine who told me to "never run in front of the soldiers. It makes them nervous." Stran did not run in front of those bulls that day, even though we were running late and had a long list of things to do. Instead, he calmed himself, made sure that his amygdala was not stacked, and entered the arena with a positive, gentle, developmental mindset. The outcome that I witnessed that day, albeit only for a few minutes, was a leadership laboratory for myself.

Whether it's teaching in the classroom, leading in the boardroom, coaching a sports team, or volunteering at the YMCA, it is a leadership laboratory where you either inspire those around you or fill them with uncertainty, fear, and anxiety. The most elite in the world start with themselves. They never want to make the people they lead nervous. Instead, they want to make them confident, challenged, and inspired.

In that brief moment, I saw a bull—in fact, I saw three bulls—who trusted the man in the arena.

Scan the QR code for bonus video content!

Bonus Video Content!

CHAPTER 13

Her Name Is Destiny

"To get somewhere I'd never been, I knew I'd have to do things I'd never done. I still had this hunger, this dream, and I knew God didn't put that desire in my heart for nothing."
–Stran T Smith

BLUF: Embrace the pain of the journey.

In December 2006, after returning from the NFR and the coincidental (or, as I believe, God-appointed) meeting with Paula White, I came home and started physical therapy on my recently reconstructed shoulder. I'd had plenty of injuries in the past and knew all about rehabbing them, but I was not prepared for what I was about to go through. One of the keys to recovery was to get my range of motion and flexibility back. This was going to be a challenge because the doctors did not think I would ever be able to swing a rope again, let alone competitively.

They took my arm out of the sling, and I held it folded in front of me. This position is what they call zero degrees. The full range of motion is 180 degrees. The goal for me was to reach 90 degrees. I was in so much pain that I couldn't imagine how this was going to happen. This was a daily routine, so

I wasn't able to see much improvement. I even left rehab every day and went home and did the exercises in the evening. I'm not sure the "cowboy mentality" was such a good thing in this case: "A little do a little good, a lot do a lot of good." But I knew deep down I would get there and do whatever it took to make it happen. After five months, I was at about 45 degrees and was cleared to start roping again.

I still had not heard from Dodd. He wasn't answering his phone, and he didn't text. Did I need to send up a smoke signal to get in touch with him? I nearly gave up on him, but I was cleared to rope, so I entered one of the top five rodeos in the state in Austin, Texas. I didn't even know if I could swing a rope. I hadn't practiced yet, but I knew I had Topper. He was my ace in the hole. The doctors had cleared me; they said my arm was attached, and I wasn't going to do any damage, but I didn't have any range of motion at all. I was like a major league pitcher, just barely pitching underhanded. I was almost side-arming the rope.

In Austin, I won second, but it wasn't because of my ability. It was because of Topper. He made up for me not being able to rope at my best. I was just throwing it out there, catching them, going down, and tying them up. Topper was just that good. He made it possible for me to win second place at that first rodeo back.

When we got home from Austin, I got a phone call, and it was Dodd. He said, "My brother, it's time." Like, okay, what does that mean? He said, "You need to fly to Miami tomorrow." So, Jennifer and I got everything packed, jumped on a plane, and flew to Miami.

We spent a couple of days there just training. In Dodd's program, you work out, eat, visit, sleep, and then start over the next day. I left out that before you sleep, you stretch. Dodd called this Stretch Class. I called it Torture. Everything he did was strategic. He had been studying roping, learning everything about it. I didn't know that he had taken this on himself. He wanted to know everything about roping—about the balance of riding, the dismount, the technique of the tie-down, and all the different muscles that were required to do what we needed to be done.

One morning, after we'd worked out, we went to the beach, and Jennifer and Dodd talked while I did some rehab out in the ocean. He asked her, "What does Stran need to accomplish this mission?"

Jennifer said, "Topper is the greatest horse ever, but he's 25 years old, and Stran doesn't want to ride him at every event. He takes care of him and will not ride him at anything but the big events. He needs another horse to ride at these other rodeos."

"Okay," Dodd said, and then he started praying for another horse for me to ride.

I didn't know any of this. After doing rehab in the ocean and eating, we went to a vitamin shop. Dodd was picking out supplements that he wanted me to take, telling me which ones to buy, and educating me on what I needed to be putting in my body. I looked over the top of the aisles and saw Jennifer, about two rows over, on her phone. I could tell from the look on her face that something was wrong. I immediately went over to her and said, "Are our boys okay?"

"Yes," she said, "our parents are good. Our family is good."

I didn't say it out loud, but I thought, "I'm good. There's nothing she can say right now that's going to really knock me off track right here." Then I asked her, "What is it?"

"Topper got out of his pen last night," she said. "He got hit by a truck, and it killed him."

I couldn't have imagined this in my wildest dreams. Topper was our pet, a part of the family. He just walked around our place. He always found my dad because my dad always had peppermints for him, and he loved peppermints. You could even feed that horse hamburger. I would have let him come into the house.

The news hit me so hard that I just walked out into the alleyway behind the vitamin shop and tried to process what I'd heard. Farther down the alley was a telephone pole, and I just knelt by that pole and started talking to the Lord.

"What? What is? What? What? How? Why? Why? That's my ace in the hole. I've been through all of this bullshit (it's probably not a good idea to cuss when you are talking to the Lord, but I'm pretty sure He understands), and all of these things I've come back from. You know, Lord, I remember—and I know You remember—when I brought him home for the first time. I stopped and unloaded him at that roadside park, and I told You, 'This is not my horse.' I gave him to You. He's Yours. The devil stole this horse. He didn't steal him from me; he stole him from You."

Then I said something that I still barely believe I would have the nerve to say: "So, what are You gonna do about it?"

Ah, man, you can imagine what kind of state of mind I was in to be talking to God like that. I cussed and called Him out.

Topper wasn't just a horse. He was a part of my family. Now, the hard part began. We all had to grieve and look for another horse that could help me achieve my goals. I didn't think I would be able to find a horse to replace Topper.

Jen and I came home a week later, and despite our grief over Topper, I knew that God had a bigger plan, so I started looking for another horse.

Finally, I found one that, like Topper, was untouchable. The family that owned this horse had sons who rodeoed. I called them and asked them if they would sell her. They knew what had happened to Topper and agreed to sell her to me because of that. Her name was Adelida. I said, "I can't call a horse Adelida," I'm a namer—I name everything—but I couldn't think of another name for her.

Later on, Jennifer was talking to Dodd on the phone and telling him about Adelida and how we did not like her name but couldn't think of anything else. He immediately said, "Her name is Destiny."

Instantly, we knew that was it. From that moment on, she was known as Destiny.

In 2007, Stran made the NFR despite only competing for half of a season due to his shoulder rehab. He knew this would probably not be the year to win, coming from so far behind and with just a few months of competing on Destiny, but after finishing second in the NFR average and fifth in the world, he knew that 2008 was shaping up to be a great one. He was playing the long game. He knew success doesn't happen overnight, and he was working with his team of Dodd and Destiny to refine his processes and strategies to win.

From the minute he started training with Dodd in 2007 until December 2008, the mindset, the situational awareness, the self-awareness, and the discipline would all lead to a magical moment that played out on TV, not only the making of a world champion at the age of 38, but the love story that was shared with the world as Jennifer found out before Stran that he was finally a world champion. What's interesting for me as a co-author of this book is that I recently learned that Dodd Romero was not there the night when Stran won the World Championship.

He was on a plane headed home. He would later tell Stran, "I did not need to be there. My work was done. I knew you would win."

Dodd could not have picked a better name for my new horse. Her name was Destiny, and it fit perfectly. I was able to buy Destiny in June 2007, but my journey with her and my transformation was just beginning. This was a new venture for me, not only physically but in every aspect, including how we traveled. Starting off, Dodd insisted on changing the way I ate and worked out, and I went from 210 pounds to 173.

I was stronger, faster, and more flexible—all the things that he said I would be. We transformed my body into a machine. He said, "Now you need to have your family with you on the road, but they need a place that's comfortable, that's home for them." So, I bought a bus—the "toterhome," which is a truck with a box on it, like a tour bus. It has more towing capacity than a regular motorhome, which is important because the trailer needed to tow the horse is heavy as well.

In a typical rodeo season, a cowboy will compete in 80–100 events per year. This means they will travel somewhere between 80,000 and 100,000 miles a year and be on the road for about 200 to 250 days.

The toterhome had five beds, a king-size bed in the back, a full bathroom, and a full kitchen so Jennifer could make meals. We even had a freezer underneath. It had a humongous picture of me on the side, along with all my sponsors. We had a 40-foot horse trailer for the horses, and it also had a huge living compartment, which we used to carry our bikes, workout bench, and weights. Everything I needed to be successful and for my family to be comfortable was right there on the road with us.

There were three TVs on that bus. We had a generator that ran everything. It always made Jennifer nervous when she drove, but she did. She was a trooper, and she knew it was important for me to get rest. That was the whole reason behind the "toterhome." This humongous bus was for us to be able to have a home wherever we were. When we removed the pop-outs, we had a WWF wrestling ring in the center of this thing, so we could wrestle, fight, and even play football. It was an amazing time for our family and the source of some of my favorite memories with my boys.

I quit going to as many rodeos as I had in the past. Instead, I focused on the bigger rodeos. This allowed me to be rested, to have the proper nutrition, and to take the time to get our workouts, cardio, and stretching in. This whole transformation didn't just happen overnight. From the time I got Destiny until the finals in 2008, it was around 18 months. When I'd rodeoed before, I'd driven all night long and sacrificed my body. I hadn't gotten the proper rest or allowed myself—or my horses—time to recover. So, this was a huge transformation.

When 2008 came around, it was my first full season with Destiny, and it was a magical time for me and my family. I didn't win every rodeo that I went to, but I was consistent in how I was rodeoing. I had a definite plan for what I was going to do, how I was going to go about my schedule, where we were going to stop, when we would eat, and how we would work out.

Before we knew it, the long days of summer had faded, and the 2008 season was over. Thanksgiving came, and then we left Childress with our sights set on Vegas. I had the boys and Jennifer with me on the bus, and Destiny was in the trailer. That's another thing. I had a four-horse trailer, but I took out all the dividers and let her have the whole trailer to herself. She had a mobile stall unit going down the road. She could walk around if she wanted to, or she could lie down.

When we pulled into Vegas, I knew that something was a little different. Well, number one, I was picking Dodd up at the airport because he was flying in from Miami. He wanted to be there.

The Finals are ten days long. It's a marathon of making appearances and doing press every day for your sponsors, signing autographs, going to mandatory meetings, and then getting your mind right to compete at the top of your game every single night. If you win a round, you have to make another appearance for the nightly awards, which will keep you up until 2 a.m. or later. If you don't win that night, you still have other sponsorship obligations to attend to. The NFR is not for the faint of heart. It's easy to get exhausted, sick, and overwhelmed if you aren't careful.

Over the 20 years of rodeoing and 15 years of competing at the National Finals, I had learned how to say no to some things. I had always had great sponsors, and I did my best to show my appreciation by showing up at every function they requested. But in 2008, I had one goal: to win a World Championship. Every decision that I made was with that in mind. I never prayed to win a World Championship; I just prayed for God's will to be done.

That was my prayer. If that was what He had for me, then that's what I wanted. If not, I was completely good with that. That didn't make me want it any less, though, I promise. From the beginning of the year to the end, my prayer was, "Let me be in the mix."

In 2008, all the number crunchers after the ninth go-round did the math, and there were six or seven guys with a chance to win the World Championship. I was one of them.

I knew I had a chance, which was all I'd asked for—just to be in the mix. Now, it was time to finish the job—go finish it, big boy. That night, I slept like a baby. Dodd had been there with me for all the previous nine performances. I still remember seeing him walk around the Thomas & Mack, up in the corridor to the very top. Once, I was standing on the arena floor, and the person next to me said, "My goodness. What is that?"

I looked up and saw Dodd, with his baggy sweats, long dreads, and sunglasses, and he was stretching. He had his leg up on the wall and was doing the splits. I said, "Oh, my. That's Dodd."

I didn't know it at the time, but on the morning of the tenth performance, Dodd and Sabina, his wife, got on a plane and went home.

In the movie *The Legend of Bagger Vance*, before Rannulph Junuh plays the last hole, his caddy, Bagger Vance, played by Will Smith, walks off of the golf course. As he leaves, the caddy looks at Junuh and says, "You don't need me anymore." That's what it was like when Dodd flew home the morning of the tenth go-round. He said, "You don't need me anymore." He was 100% confident that I was going to win the World Championship.

Now, this was not by any stretch of the imagination a done deal. I was not in the lead. I needed to do well in the tenth go-round, and I also needed to win the average to be the world champion. I needed to win about $50,000 on the last day to pull it off.

As I was driving to the Thomas & Mack Center that night with my family, like I had done a hundred times before through the years, my dad, ever the conservative, said to me, "You know, you've got third in the average won if you just get a time. So, if something happens, just make sure you get a time." Third in the average paid about $20,000. It wasn't that my dad didn't want me to win or didn't think I could do it… he's just an old-school kind of guy. He didn't want me to go so hard after first that I gambled away the safe $20,000 I'd win if I just went out and had a solid, complete run. I knew he meant well, but that was not what I was there for.

We were sitting at a red light, so I looked at my dad and said, "If somebody walked up to me right now and said, 'We're going to give you $20,000,' do you know what I would do? I would take the money, and I would throw it out the window. It's not about the money anymore. I've got one goal, and that's it. I'm leaving with that gold buckle."

I knew that I needed to win this go-round or, at worst, get second. I also knew that the calf I drew that night would really challenge me, but I had Destiny, and she was a difference-maker. It was like Destiny knew when it was a high-pressure situation. I could just feel her collect herself and zone in. I remember riding her in the box that night when it was my turn to compete. You've probably heard people talk about "being in the zone." Well, I can't ever remember a time in my life when I was more "in the zone" than right then. I really couldn't hear anything. I had tunnel vision. I can still remember the way my rope smelled. Time actually slowed down for me. I was so ultra-focused.

The calf came out of the chute, and I got a great start. She stepped to the right, which is one of those things that's not always the best, especially if they're running hard, but I was sitting on a rocket ship. Destiny could run like the wind, and she tore the ground up. I threw my rope out a little further than I would normally have been comfortable throwing for a World Championship, but it was a gold buckle or bust for me. My entire professional career had come down to this run. I knew exactly what I had to do, and I did it.

When I threw my hands up and the clock stopped, suddenly, I was conscious again. As I climbed back on Destiny, I could hear the crowd roaring, and I thought, "Oh, my gosh. What have I just done?" I counted in my head, "One-one thousand, two-one thousand, three-one thousand…"

When the six seconds were up, and I knew I was safe, I screamed as loudly as I could, and that's really not like me. I looked at the clock—7.2.

The time held, and I won the average. Even with five guys left to rope, none of them would be able to catch me in the aggregate. This meant I was guaranteed to win the NFR—but the World Championship was still up in the air, depending on how the last five ropers did. I took that moment, though, to just savor the moment of winning the NFR Average.

Typically, after each event, the world champion is announced right away. This year, the numbers were so close that the officials had to calculate and recalculate to be sure. I'd been here before, in 2004, so I wasn't going to let the question of the World Championship rob me of the joy of winning the NFR.

I got back on Destiny and made the victory lap for the NFR average, still not knowing if I'd won the World Championship. After they announce the average winners following each event, they present the trophy saddle in the arena, so I walked out to receive my saddle and take a picture with the commissioner and the sponsors. The next stop for the average winners after getting their saddle is to go to the sideline TV interview.

For years, the sideline reporter was my wife. While I was out competing, she didn't get to sit in the stands or be behind the scenes like the other wives—she was doing her own job. Jennifer was stationed just outside the arena, and that year, for the first time, the tenth round was being broadcast live on ESPN. In the past, it was live to tape, so there was a delay. As I got close to the gate, I saw Jennifer, and I could tell just by looking at her that I had won the World Championship.

Now, Jennifer has always been a consummate professional. No matter what was happening to me or our family members, win or lose, you'd never be able to tell by watching her on TV. That night, though... that night, she couldn't hold back her excitement and jumped into my arms. I just kept saying, "Are you sure? Are you sure?"

The statistician Bob Welch, a production manager at PRCA, is a family friend and was a part of my journey. He watched this whole thing. I looked at him, and he confirmed everything. I couldn't believe it, as you can see in the ESPN interview. Jennifer says it's one of her worst interviews ever. I think it's the best one she's ever done. The cool thing for us is we were live, so it was all caught on camera. We were both nearly speechless.

As I stood there, all of a sudden, time slowed down again. I saw Shawn. I saw Topper. I saw that shower floor in Boston. I saw my granddad. I thought of all those sleepless nights that I'd had, the times I lay on my back in the middle of the arena with the lights on, the only one around, just bleeding and crying. I saw all of that, and I prayed, "Lord, give me some words here. Just whatever you want me to say."

The words that came out of my mouth were, "It just goes to show, never give up. Never give up on your dream. All I know is that God's not just good once in a while. He's good all the time. If you're still out there and your heart's still beating, it's proof that God's not through with you yet. You don't have to win a gold buckle to fulfill your purpose. So, never give up. Don't ever give up on your dreams."

It was only one gold buckle, but it made such an impact. People tell me all the time that they remember that moment, and it's their favorite NFR memory. More than that, the gold buckle has opened doors for me to be able to share not only what I've learned in rodeo but how to apply those principles to everyday life. It's allowed me to impact and speak life into thousands of young kids who have a dream just like I did. Maybe one of them will be inspired by this to write their own book one day, tell their story, and have an impact far beyond what I've done.

My favorite moment in all of rodeo was hearing I'd won a World Championship from my wife after all we'd been through together. I can't really put into words what that meant to us—and what it still means to me today. She really was my destiny.

As crazy as this all sounds, I'd never picked these things to happen the way they did. I always felt like I should have won the gold buckle before 2008. If you didn't know any better, you would have thought my best chances of winning it had come and gone. By 2008, most people would have expected me to be announcing my retirement. At that point, I'd had six surgeries and gone through what should have been two career-ending medical events.

Destiny was a great horse, but I'd had others that were just as good: Topper, Piggybank, Rifleman, Whoa… Some of the all-time greatest tie-down roping horses in history came through my barn, but I never won a World Championship on them. The Colonel and I wouldn't be writing this book right now if I had.

Despite my relentless pursuit of my goal, I wasn't chasing the World Championship for the sake of being a champion. It was to live out God's purpose for my life at the highest level and to know that my true identity would never depend on a gold buckle or the lack of one. I would have never chosen this path, which has been full of loss, heartache, and pain, but if I could go back and change things, I wouldn't. It has made me the man I am today. The pain of the distance was worth the price of the journey.

For Stran Smith, the path to winning a gold buckle was not only unique and rare; it was elite. It may never be replicated again. From his early 20s to the age of 38, he was invested in a leadership laboratory, one filled with setbacks, loss, injuries, a stroke, and the birth of children. It should not have happened. At any time during those 15 years, Stran could have ridden off into the sunset and still been considered a success story. How many rodeo cowboys have been featured in *European GQ*, listed as one of *People* magazine's Most Eligible Bachelors, been a spokesmodel for international brands, and been successful ropers? He had a supportive wife, great kids, and a comfortable life in Childress, Texas. His life was full without the World Championship.

When Stran and I decided to write this book several years ago, I had only just learned what it took to win a World Championship. The mindset of the elite is rare. The elite never arrive. Every experience is an opportunity to develop, rep character, and try another way. A loss is a lesson. It's never punitive; it's developmental. Faith, family, friends, community, teams, and self—six causes for which each of us has the opportunity to serve.

What's required to become a man or woman of character who wins remains the same. It's situational awareness, self-awareness, and the courage (heart) to take action when most will not. It's the fear of ego creeping into the equation. It's choosing the harder right over the easier wrong. Leadership can be lonely. Throughout those 15 years on the path to the gold buckle, most of that time was spent either alone or in the company of one to four people. However, Stran would finish in front of thousands.

For the lead-up, however, no one was in the stands cheering, telling him, "Congratulations! You got needed rest and nutrition. Your hydration was perfect today." The elite recognize that the most important development is going to come in times when they're alone. Coach Nick Saban said, "If you truly want to become great, you don't have many choices." To become *elite* is even rarer. There's no doubt that the story of Stran and Jennifer Smith, along with Dodd Romero, deserves to be told on the big screen.

Stran should have never won the gold buckle, but he overcame extraordinary circumstances and did exactly that. Mission, Mindset, Process. This… is a story of destiny.

Scan the QR code for bonus video content!

Bonus Video Content!

Conclusion
(Chapter 14)

> *"As a baseball player, we simply can't have 13 Chapters. Therefore, I declare that our Conclusion is our last chapter. This is **Chapter 14!**"*
> —J. Craig Flowers

Readers, if you've made it this far, first of all, we thank you! But more than that, be proud of yourself. Picking up a book like this means you are committed to your personal growth, being an elite leader, and the pursuit of excellence.

Often, people think about leadership as only being for the few who are in positions of command or authority: military officers, like the Colonel, church deacons like Stran, C-suite managers, coaches, team captains, and such. But leadership, simply put, is service to a cause. Leadership is all around us, whether we think of ourselves as leaders or not. You might be a self-employed introvert, but you can still be an elite leader! Even if we lead no one else, we must lead ourselves.

What does it mean, exactly, to lead yourself? In short, it means choosing the harder right over the easier wrong. It means trying today, tomorrow, and every day that follows to be the best version of yourself. We all have a mission in our lives. Some call it a calling; others call it a purpose. Whatever you call it, it's up to each of us not only to accept it but to decide how we are going to choose to show up for it, even when we're by ourselves. Especially when we're by ourselves. We hope one of your takeaways from this book is seeing that the elite become that way from behaviors, not talent.

Throughout this book, we've discussed mission, mindset, and process. It's not enough to just have a mission or a goal. The elite approach their mission with the right mindset. When challenges come our way—and they will for every single one of us—the elite have learned how to get their minds in the right place to execute the mission. They practice character reps and train to choose the harder right. Choosing the easy path is what usually feels natural to us, but choosing to embrace the hard is what sets the elite apart. Mindset involves situational awareness, self-awareness, and discipline, all of which must precede action. Mindset means you are fully committed to your mission, but you are also not driven by emotions.

The process can be summed up as the journey. It's important to remember not to get so focused on the goal that you forget the beauty of the process. You fall in love with that, not the end destination. It would be easy to read Stran's story and think that he was driven to win a gold buckle, but that was just the result of a process he fell in love with. The time he got to spend on his process—the workouts, the practice, the traveling with his family—was the thing that drove him to keep going.

If you aren't careful, accomplishments, accolades, fame, and trophies can become a distraction rather than a goal. The process is getting to do your mission, your calling, your purpose. Falling in love with the process helps keep your mindset positive when you're hit with frustration, discouragement, or negativity.

Stran said this once already in this book, but it's worth repeating because his words are every bit as relevant today as they were on that December night in 2008:

"Never give up on your dream. All I know is that God's not just good once in a while. He's good all the time. If you're still out there and your heart's still beating, it's proof that God's not through with you yet. You don't have

to win a gold buckle to fulfill your purpose. So, don't ever give up on your dreams."

CONTINUE YOUR JOURNEY WITH STRAN AND THE COLONEL

Stran and the Colonel reached the pinnacle of their careers in roping and military service, but now their missions have evolved. The elite are never finished; they are always pursuing their next goal, purpose, and calling. The elite are content but never satisfied. The best will always be yet to come. For Stran and the Colonel, that mission is sharing what they've learned and helping others become, find, and pursue their mission and become elite at whatever it is they are called to do. Their podcast, *A Colonel & A Cowboy (with a little bit of Jen)*, will launch in 2025, and the two will also continue their speaking events and leadership training. To keep up with them or to book one or both of them at your event, visit their website at www.acolonelandacowboy.com.

A SPECIAL THANKS

To Kellie Carr-Augustyn:
Your invaluable work was instrumental in the swift completion of this book.
Thank you for being an integral part of the journey.

Rodeo Glossary

Thank you to the Professional Rodeo Cowboys Association for providing this guide to learn more about Stran's event, Tie-Down Roping, and the sport of rodeo. Visit www.prorodeo.com for more information.

Tie-down roping - To start this sprinting event, the tie-down roper and his horse back into the box; the cowboy carries a rope in one hand and a "piggin' string" in his mouth. When the cowboy nods, the chute opens and the calf gets a head start. The cowboy throws a loop over its head; his horse stops and pulls the rope taut while the cowboy jumps off, dashes down the rope, lays the calf on the ground and uses the piggin' string to tie any three of its legs together. Then he lifts his hands to show he is finished, and the field flag judge drops a flag to stop the clock. The horse is trained to keep the rope taut until the cowboy remounts and moves the horse toward the calf, giving the rope slack. If the calf's legs stay tied correctly for six seconds, it's a qualified run and the time stands.

Average - Usually used to describe the aggregate score for a contestant who competed in more than one round. For example, "He had times of 9.3 and 9.8 seconds in the two rounds and placed third in the average with 19.1 seconds on two head."

Barrier - In timed events, a line at the front of the box that the contestant and his horse cannot cross until the steer or calf has a head start, usually marked with a rope and a flag so the timers can see it drop and start the clock.

Box - In a timed event, the area a horse and rider back into before they make a roping or steer wrestling run Breaking the barrier: in the timed events, if the rider leaves the box too soon – failing to give the animal enough of a head start – he is assessed a 10-second penalty.

Calf roper - A tie-down roper.

Chute - A pen that holds an animal safely in position.

Draw - Each timed-event contestant is assigned a calf or steer in a random draw on-site, shortly before each performance of a rodeo begins.

Finals/NFR/WNFR - The Wrangler National Finals Rodeo, often abbreviated to "NFR/WNFR" or simply "The Finals." This is rodeo's Super Bowl, or world championship. It is held every December, and is 10 rounds of competition. The NFR has been held in several cities throughout the U.S., but has been in Las Vegas since 1985, with the exception of 2020, when it was temporarily moved to Arlington, Texas, due to COVID-19.

Gold Buckle - A coveted trophy belt buckle won by World Champions in the Professional Rodeo Cowboys Association. Often used interchangeably with "world champion." For instance, "he was chasing a gold buckle" is the same as saying, "he was chasing a world championship."

Go-round - Many rodeos have more than one round of competition; each is called a go-round, and all cowboys entered in that rodeo compete in each go-round unless there is a semi-final, final or progressive round.

Hooey - The knot that a cowboy uses to finish tying the calf's legs together in tie-down roping.

Piggin' string - In tie-down roping, the small rope used to tie a calf's legs together.

Rookie - a cowboy in his first year of card-holding PRCA membership.

Rope - The correct term is rope, not lasso, lariat or riata; most ropes used in ProRodeo timed events are made of strong yet flexible braided materials such as nylon/poly blends, and a cowboy may change his rope selection depending on the weather and the cattle.

Slack - Excess entries at some rodeos may be scheduled for preliminary (slack) competition, usually before the rodeo opens to the public.

Standings - A professional cowboy's success is measured in earnings, and cowboys may keep track of where they rank in yearly earnings in several sets of standings.

World Champion - The PRCA cowboy who has won the most money overall for the year in their event. Includes regular season earnings and earnings from the National Finals Rodeo.

THANK YOU FOR READING OUR BOOK!

DOWNLOAD YOUR FREE GIFTS

Just to say thanks for buying and reading our book, we would like to give you a few free bonus items!

Scan the QR Code:

We appreciate your interest in our book and value your feedback as it helps us improve future versions of this book. We would appreciate it if you could leave your invaluable review on Amazon.com with your feedback. Thank you!

www.ingramcontent.com/pod-product-compliance
Lightning Source LLC
Chambersburg PA
CBHW030242010526
44107CB00030B/1309/J